ARE YOU BEING SET UP TO FAIL?

Jillion R. Rising

Are You Being Set Up to Fail?
Copyright © 2018 by Jillion R.Rising

ISBN (Print Edition): 978-1-54393-086-3
ISBN (eBook Edition): 978-1-54393-087-0

Preface

Are you feeling as though the burdens or problems you face are insurmountable and beyond finding a solution? Do you have the sensation of helplessness, thinking *"What's the use, everything I care about has a predetermined outcome controlled by others?"* You are not alone; this sensation of hopelessness has become an integral part of many Americans' way of thinking.

As we progress through each chapter, we're going to strategically shine a light on the sources that are responsible for the hopelessness you feel. Additionally, through careful steps we're going to rekindle a sensation of optimism by helping you understand a power that already exists within you, thus providing you with the confidence you need to control your destiny to a brighter future.

As we continue, you will learn things about yourself using a method that has not been used before. Regardless of your struggles, what follows is a clear path to mental health uniquely designed to provide answers to every individual reader. This book is not filled with the typical jargon of psychiatric medicine...it is specifically designed to help each individual reader learn how to uniquely change his or her life!

The title, "Are you Being Set Up to Fail?" implies a question to you the reader. In what follows I intend to provide the answer to this question, believing that once you hear what I have to say you will come to the same conclusion I have, which is an emphatic yes, you can change!

Table of Contents

Introduction

This is a book about the *mental health* of America, exposing how our *political system* along with the *mass media* have collectively impacted us as citizens. Almost everywhere we look within American society, it has become apparent that our expectations as a people have reached an all-time low, with many of our citizens finding it difficult to feel they've achieved success in anything. As we continue, we're going to discuss the overabundance of moving parts and distractions happening within our daily lives, helping you to step back and look at your existence from the outside in. My intent is to help you become aware of the obstacles that are preventing you from living a life of satisfaction.

Each morning people wake up all over America and start their day by turning on their television, laptop, or any other form of communication they may use in order to update what they may have missed during the night. Many Americans have remained in a constant state of alert after experiencing the horrific attack on New York's twin towers along with the subsequent attacks that have followed here and around the world. There's no question that people around the world are concerned about whether they will wake up to yet another tragedy. I believe the terrorist attacks, along with the advancement of technology, have brought us to a *constant state of crisis* through the delivery of sensationalized news; the media has become an *"enemy of the state"* as far as the mental health and well-being of our families.

America is supposed to be the land of the free, but we seem to be trapped in systems that limit our freedoms and alter how we think about them. In other words, television has become the driving force of mass propaganda, delivering messaging to you in every aspect of your life. Whether the media is either knowingly or unknowingly instilling fear, using their messaging to create a **constant crisis or state of fear,** is something we will analyze. What I hope to make clear during our time together is how this *state of crisis/fear* is being used to achieve change on a massive scale to our country's basic culture of offering freedom to all people.

Additionally, we will discuss how and why the *mass media* has used the art of advertising to **"sell you an experience,"** creating for its viewers the feeling that their lives have not been fulfilled unless they do whatever *experience is being advertised.* From this onslaught of advertising, many people start collecting *mental bucket lists* of these so-called *experiences,* causing them to feel anxious or restless, giving them the feeling that their lives are boring and a nagging feeling that they are missing out. We will also discuss how network programming has collectively decided to give you, the **"viewer,"** programs of dysfunction, and how these programs have lowered the moral standards and expectations of America's families.

Technology and the onslaught of social media are here to stay, but as a *nation* full of educated people we must decide how we can best use it. We must pay attention and understand the dangers within the messaging our families receive, deciding what they should view by understanding the potential impact it may have upon our children's lives. My hope is that we can find common ground as collective citizens, working together to pursue the betterment of our families by discussing ideas to achieve happiness within our *mental state of mind.* In the following chapters I carefully build this case, drawing your attention to the *subliminal messages* we receive daily that are designed to sell products regardless of their damaging effects on you and your family!

About the Author

Much of my life has been spent empowering others, so speaking about myself is not something I find easy to do. I do realize it is important for me to disclose who I am, since I'm asking you to donate your valuable time to reading my book. I cannot mention a word about myself without thanking the people I have had the pleasure of team building with during my 35 years of managing. As you begin to understand the perspective presented in this book, you will begin to realize the importance I place on growing as a person through the communication with others.

My career started in the trenches of America's working class… always doing my best to learn each job to the best of my abilities. I was fortunate that my employers recognized my leadership skills and allowed me the opportunity to be a part of managing their business. My strength within the management team was having the ability to see special *gifts* within other employees. I learned early on that my ability to identify what came easy to other people empowered my own *gift,* which was and still is the ability to help others achieve excellence in their job performance.

For the last 25 years I've owned and operated a multi-million-dollar business employing thousands of people. The unexpected benefit I received throughout my years of managing was learning that the problems I thought were uniquely my own were commonly shared by many other people. The process of managing employees but also helping them as people became medicine for my own mental health.

I cannot stress enough to those who suffer and believe they are alone with the burdens they carry that I am here to deliver the good news:

you are not alone! I have spent a lifetime helping people achieve limits they thought were beyond their reach. In most cases it is not the circumstances we are born in that limits our ability to grow. In almost every case I've learned it is generally the restrictions or limitations we place upon ourselves that prevent us from living a satisfying existence.

Thank you for allowing me to share my wealth of experience with you. Together we can change the way we feel about ourselves and how we perceive others. I am certain as you continue to read, you will begin to understand why I believe you *will become a better you!*

CHAPTER 1

You Are Not Crazy!

As I watch the daily news media, I find it appalling that they are constantly portraying Americans as a directionless people in need of assistance. I've invested countless hours managing and learning what is happening in the lives of people, and what I almost always find to be the common denominator is confusion and lack of trust from the mixed messaging they receive from the people presently running our country. We see media reporters visiting college campuses and giving us distorted coverage, displaying young Americans as if they are completely incapable of governing themselves. This outlook paints America's future as bleak.

What I say to the media in response to their arrogance directed toward America's citizens is, *"You are what you eat."* Many of you can relate to this phrase because we've become more educated about the food we eat, carefully reading the labels when making our selection because we know America's corporations are lacing their prepackaged food with chemicals. The response to our demands for safer food has caused a movement within the food industry to provide organically grown foods in our supermarkets and grocery stores. There are scores of citizens planting their own gardens at home in order to ensure they can trust the food they are consuming. My goal is to help you understand that as careful as we've become with selecting our food, we must use the same caution when digesting the *mass media* and their daily messaging. *"You are what you eat"* also applies to the information and messaging we digest.

It greatly troubles me to see the negative portrayal of America by the *mass media* when it is they who are responsible for the mixed messaging presented to our families daily! We can compare our media to the junk food industry; just as we've seen the overabundance of garbage food, we have also seen an overabundance of junk television programing, journalism, and political propaganda. How many of us enter the local grocery store for the purpose of buying soap or maybe shampoo and end up leaving the aisle in a complete state of confusion because of the plethora of different brands, all of them claiming to be better than the other! There is no doubt that we have become inundated with new products, fashion, and the ever-changing technological devices.

My message to you as fellow citizens is to stress the importance for us to be aware that we are collectively being inundated with junk food, junk media, and dysfunctional television programs. The cause and effect of this onslaught have put our bodily systems receiving this **mass messaging** on overload! I ask that you take a moment to consider how many times a day do you feel anxiety starting to creep in as a result of the plethora of choices available to you in products, clothing, or technology…leaving you with the feeling that you must rush to make a choice, to pick something?

My top priority is to help you understand **you are not crazy!** Who the hell wouldn't have anxiety given all the choices and who wouldn't start believing we're a bunch of misfits after seeing nothing but dysfunctional television programs delivered to us daily? Please pause and consider the messaging we receive from what I refer to as the *advertisers of evil* on how they believe Americans should deal with our anxiety. They flood us with advertisements attempting to sell us an overload of drugs helping to calm our nerves, stop depression, and help us sleep; this list goes on and on! Once they coerce you into using these so-called healing drugs designed to help you solve your problems, it is then that we see advertisements from law firms also advertising on television stating the drugs you've been using are known to cause cancer, heart failure, or possibly seizures!

I ask you to put aside emotion and continue with me using *good old fashioned* logic to dissect the process of mass media, and together we will learn how and why America has come to a state of dysfunction. The important thing to understand is that we are not a weak and confused people and that we are not crazy individuals in constant need of drugs and counseling. We must put our lives on pause and review who is navigating this great ship known throughout the world as America.

There is an old and somewhat crude phrase, but I believe it applies: *"the pig rots from the head and not the tail."* This phrase has been used throughout history when a source of leadership (in this case our government) has been corrupted through greed and power, often selling the soul of its citizens. The American people go to work every day, with their children doing their part by going to school and getting an education; so it is clear that the *"tail"* (reference to the pig) is doing their part. Our government has the responsibility to captain the ship, and similar to the sinking of the *Titanic,* they have rammed us into a psychological iceberg!

As we continue, I will explain why I believe much of our network programing displaying *dysfunction* upon our television sets is intentional. My hope is to gain your trust and understanding. The only agenda I have is for America to remain a free-spirited nation, driven by a cause of unity and positive mental health. We must remember America's citizens are what made this a great country, and without them collectively working together as one people, being of *healthy mind and healthy spirit,* we cannot continue to be the inspiration representing the value of a free society to the world.

My plan is to present logic, helping you to decode the subliminal messaging we receive, learn who is sending the messaging, and finally what these messengers have to gain. My goal is to highlight the importance of protecting your mental health and your rights as citizens, ultimately creating a sense of well-being for you the reader. My only fear is whether we can get honest representation within our government to help make good choices before we continue too far along with the present path of destruction.

If we analyze our *mass media*, their goal appears to be becoming the leading network viewed here in America and throughout the world. We must be crystal clear with our understanding: the goal for every network is to achieve a vast viewership, knowing the grand prize for their large viewership is to obtain sponsors willing to spend mega advertising dollars on their network. This process is important for you understand, because the media shows little integrity when choosing their advertisers, also known as sponsors. They do not care what misinformation the sponsor carries within their background or the danger their product may bring to the overall mental or physical health of our people. The decisions they make are based on generating clients who are willing to spend money advertising on their network, no matter what the product.

Finally, we should understand that the media networks have decided that bizarre behavior and sensationalism are what bring more viewers to their network. Most of them become guilty of walking the line between delivering what we call tabloid gossip compared to real news. If our networks continue to produce nothing more than sensationalism and bizarre dysfunctional "news" as normal, how will our children be able to decipher what is truthful reporting and what is sensational fiction? It is upon us the viewers to decide if we will remain the lab rats for the *media scientist*…allowing them the dominance to control our minds and our mental health through the use of subliminal messaging. Or will you join the fight for sanity, delivering our own subliminal message: ***the value of the information we receive matters as much as the food we eat!***

CHAPTER 2

INFORMATION OVERLOAD

I've titled this book "Are You Being Set Up to Fail" because when you take a step back and analyze our daily lives in America, I believe you will reach a similar conclusion to the one I have. What the American people must decide is if the media overload we face in our daily lives is happening because of the growth of our nation or are we being overloaded in order to keep us distracted from profound changes happening within our country.

During my life growing up in America, there were a multitude of Rock Bands creating music and lyrics explaining the tragic conditions of many citizen's lives. Some of the lyrics referred to the drugs plaguing American society, with groups producing songs such as *The Rolling Stones* *("Mother's Little Helper", or Steppenwolf ("God Damn the Pusher Man")*. Others created lyrics to shine a light on the atrocities of war, such as *Black Sabbath ("War Pigs") or John Lennon's* dream of... *("Imagine")*. Last, as we reflect on the changing fast pace of our American culture, we realize the brilliance of the *Eagles' song ("Life in the Fast Lane")*.

The discussion we will have throughout this book will shed light on why so many people within our nation are struggling to survive. If we focus our attention on the messaging of the musician's lyrics, we begin to realize that many of them have the ability to brilliantly lay out the things that plague our society. My intention is to give you examples throughout this book, helping you see through the fog of distraction, helping you to understand that in many cases we are in fact living the lives of the musicians' lyrics!

As a young man, I received advice from an older gentleman who used the phrase: *"Believe none of what you hear, little of what you read, and all of what you see."* I believe this old adage is more relevant today than any time within our country's history. I was born in 1960, and during my adolescence we were given few choices of clothing, shoes, or television programs…needless to say, life was relatively simple. Many of the folks born in the early 60's will remember that there was little choice of newspapers or magazines and depending on where your residence was located in relation to the highest antenna tower, the reception of your television's analog signal is how clarity was brought to the picture on your television tube. The younger readers will be amazed to hear we had five television channels, 2, 5, 7, 9, and 11, and later on channel 32 joined the lineup!

The last part of my friend's advice, *"believe all of what you see,"* has also become difficult to follow because of the media's ability to edit **what we see.** It has become abundantly clear that we must listen to the news cautiously as we find that many of our news agencies have become guilty of editing or sensationalizing stories for the sole purpose of advancing their agenda. By delivering news with ideological intent, they can alter outcomes favorable to advancing their agenda. Many have become victims of the media's messaging because of the overload of information, which alters our sensitivity and causes confusion about the value of truth. This has left many of us with the feeling of hopelessness and the belief that there is nothing we can do as individuals to change the process.

As we find ourselves inundated with an overabundance of news, advertisements, and political commentary along with a plethora of consumer goods available at shopping malls or Internet super stores, I pose the question whether if this overload is causing a state of confusion, especially among the older population who have grown up in a time of far fewer choices. My concern is whether this overabundance has caused us to become a nation burdened with overindulgence as part of our culture.

Additionally, if we compare the overabundance of products available to the overwhelming amount of information from written and social media, I am left with the thought of how we will be able to decipher the reality of misinformation or half-truths coming at us minute by minute on a daily basis. If the desire to provide the public with truth is no longer the driving force of our news media or Internet search engines, this leaves us asking ourselves "What is truth?" If every question and/or opinion on any given subject is nullified by another question/opinion, where does that leave us on reaching a conclusion based on truth?

We must educate ourselves about understanding the importance of our media's providing our news honestly and without bias. From America's inception, our founders understood the importance and the necessity of establishing a free press based on integrity, always relying on journalism to report incidents as they truly happened. The importance of maintaining a free press was specifically designed as one of the pillars of the protection of our nation's freedom. The founders had the foresight to understand that as America grew, its citizens would need the protection that journalists could provide if they were allowed to honestly report atrocities or unlawful events and other potential dangers capable of bringing harm to a free society. During the formation of journalism, reporters were expected to uphold the highest levels of ethical standards. The written word had a profound effect on one's reputation, and it was used to keep the public informed in developed and non-developed communities.

Unfortunately, what Americans are receiving today is a minute-by-minute sensationalized, polarized, propagandized media tsunami! Much of what we get from journalism has become slanted propaganda, divided into partisan politics using newsworthy events to sell a journalist's/network's ideological viewpoint. Remember the earlier statement, *"believe none of what you hear, little of what you read, and all of what you see."* If we do not demand integrity and assurance from our journalists that the news we receive is without bias, we will have lost one of the major pillars of the foundation of freedom in America.

It is important to realize that our country's entry into what is referred to as a technological revolution will either lift our nation into a state of unity far beyond past achievements or will divide us into a nation beyond repair. What should concern every citizen is the attempt by our politicians along with the *mass media,* driven by the *corporate elite,* to use technology to divide our citizenship into segmented groups. If we continue to allow their divide and conquer strategy by grouping citizens into what the politicians refer to as a voting base (citizens placed into identity groups labeling them as favoring either republican or democrat) then we will have allowed them to destroy what has been our strength as a country: ***"Unity."***

My grave concern regarding the *divide and conquer* strategy is the effect it has on reducing the strength of our unity while directly empowering the people *(politicians)* who divide us. As we continue to shed light on the distractions placed upon you, it is my hope that we will come together as ***united citizens*** conducting our own music and writing our own lyrics as a mentally stable citizenship controlling the fate of our communities and our country!

CHAPTER 3

HOLLYWOOD...
THE VOICE OF REASON?

T here are two places that immediately come to my mind as a danger
to the health and wellbeing of our communal stability...Hollywood
and Las Vegas! Yet it has become popular for the dysfunctional Hollywood
elite to saturate our society with their opinions in an attempt to somehow
promote their dysfunctional lives as normal. Additionally, we are inundated with commercials selling the sins of Las Vegas as *"What happens in
Vegas stays in Vegas."* I believe there are many suffering families throughout America that know firsthand what happened in Vegas did not stay
there. There are many who lost a normal family member to gambling,
alcohol, or maybe a porn addiction that has forever damaged their lives.

America has reached a boiling point where we must make tough
choices in order to ensure the mental health of our children along with
the health of our country. The first amendment to the Constitution allows
us the freedom of speech along with the freedom of expression. There
is a danger or movement developing within our country that entails a
destructive silencing of our first amendment right. We are seeing an attack
in which one group controlling a large audience is able to speak freely

promoting their ideals while silencing those they disagree with through the use of what we now refer to as *political correctness,* also known as *PC.*

I've titled this chapter with a reference to Hollywood in order to shed light on the dysfunctional *Global Goofballs,* as they seem to have pushed themselves to become the *"voice of reason"* within our lives. . Yet if we break down the essence of these *Global Goofballs* we need not travel far to see the dysfunction and confusion within the *few* families that actually exist within their community. It is not irregular for the Hollywood elites to have a child psychiatrist counseling their children on a regular basis. What has been talked about for many years and recently exposed to the public is that in order to advance their careers, many of these actors or actresses were subjected to sexual harassment or abuse. What is sad is that this abuse has been considered as industry standard, thus accepted by many as a prerequisite to career advancement within their chosen profession.

We should remember that Hollywood is full of people that spend the majority of their lives playing a role of someone other than themselves. Many of these people have been creative all their lives but have never really understood the basis of a "normal" existence because it has been their life's goal to entertain others through the portrayal of many characters. It is not my intent to minimize their value as people or to society, but we should not be considering them as models of mental stability.

We've discussed the Hollywood actors and actresses, and now we should look at the people running the show behind the scenes. These people are the ultimate puppet masters, as we have recently learned from the disclosure of the Harvey Weinstein abuse story. These people are also the creators of the television network programing as well as the choice of movies we receive for our families' viewing!

We should analyze how these creators of dysfunction obtained the power they have over the actors/actresses, our politicians, and finally you, the American public. If you recall at the beginning of this chapter I mentioned Las Vegas and Hollywood as the two places I felt brought the biggest source of danger and dysfunction to our families.

In order for Las Vegas and Hollywood to thrive, it was critical to discredit, reduce the influence of, and remove and destroy religion in America. If the majority of our citizens are bound to the moral restrictions of religion feeling burdened with the idea of judgment for their sins, this could put both Hollywood and Vegas out of business. There has been a collective effort by our government, the media, advertising, and the programs they deliver to us through network television to slowly breakdown the moral structure of the American family all for the sake of selling products and making a profit.

If we analyze the shows delivered to us from television network programmers and Hollywood movie producers, we see that the programs or movies they flood us with depict dysfunction as the norm. Many older folks probably remember the transition from the normal talk shows such as Merv Griffin to the dysfunction of the Jerry Springer program or of Dr. Phil displaying to viewers some of the more disturbed misfits of society. The intent of these shows was to display to the public that there were far more dregs within our society than we had previously thought of or been exposed to. For some, watching these shows gave them a sense of empowerment as they began to think *at least I'm not as bad as those people!* In other words, the promotion of these shows may have seemed harmless in the beginning, but what they accomplished was the start of the process of lowering the standards or expectations of America's citizens.

I am certain that some of you read the last paragraph thinking "come on, how stupid do you think we are?" To be clear, I don't think any of you are stupid...my belief is that the constant subliminal messaging delivered to us through these television shows has slowly deteriorated the fabric of a moral society, and I do not believe it is by accident. In other word I believe *"you are being set up to fail!"*

I would like to better explain my earlier statement that politicians are included in this hostile takeover of lowering the moral foundation of the American family unit. The following information came directly from the FCC (Federal Communication Commission) website. My purpose for including this short segment of FCC information is to demonstrate that our government is involved in our television programing as well as using the rules they secure for themselves for the purpose of reducing the cost of air time for political campaigning. The following are a few examples of a question/answer segment located on the FCC website.

Q: Does the FCC regulate the content of cable programming?

A: Cable television system operators generally make their own selection of channels and programs to be distributed to subscribers in response to consumer demands. The Commission does, however, have rules in some areas that are applicable to programming -- called "origination cablecast-ing" in the rules -- that are subject to the editorial control of the cable system operator. The rules generally do not apply to the content of broadcast channels or to access channels over which the cable system operator has no editorial control.

Q: How much can a cable system charge political candidates for advertising?

A: Cable television systems can only charge political candidates the "lowest unit charge of the station" for the same class and amount of time for the same period during the 45 days preceding a primary or runoff election, and 60 days preceding a general or special election. Candidates should be charged no more per unit than the system charges its most favored commercial advertisers for the same classes and amounts of time for the same periods. Information concerning the rates, terms, conditions and all discounts and privileges offered to commercial advertisers should be disclosed and made available to candidates.

Q: Can a cable system endorse or oppose a political candidate in an editorial?

A: Yes, as long as it complies with the political editorial rule. The rule requires the cable system to give to the opposing candidates not endorsed or the opposing candidate the following within 24 hours of a political editorial: (1) notification and identification of the editorial, (2) a script or tape of the editorial, and (3) an offer of a reasonable opportunity for the candidate or his or her spokesperson to respond over the cable facilities. Where an editorial is cablecast within 72 hours prior to election day, the cable system is obliged to give notice and an opportunity to respond sufficiently far enough in advance to enable the candidate opposed or not endorsed a reasonable opportunity to prepare a response and to present it in a timely fashion.

What this example demonstrates is how our federal government is clearly involved in the rules and regulations regarding the allowable content within the programming (or shows) we receive from cable networks. It also demonstrates that our government is critically involved when it comes to negotiations regarding their use of the cable networks for the benefit *(or cost)* of political advertising. Our imaginations can run wild when we consider the *favors* that may develop if one hand washes the other when government politicians are in need of a messaging system in order for the public to know who they are. Additionally, if we view this from the powerful networks perspective that spends large amounts of money lobbying politicians in an attempt to receive favor. The importance of finding and keeping politicians that will play ball becomes critically important to the *media giant* those who cooperate remain in power!

Let's continue *connecting the dots* in order to demonstrate how we are *being set up to fail.* When forming America under this concept of freedom, it was a different time and a different place. The process began from a people seeking freedom from the rule of a brutal government, along with the overpowering taxation it had placed upon its citizens. Additionally, these earlier settlers fled from the persecution imposed upon them regarding their choice of religion. The atrocities carried out against citizens for their belief in a different form of Christianity is beyond comprehension in comparison to today's tolerance of the many different denominations.

What transpired from this *fight for freedom* was the greatest country on earth, creating a government that actually worked for and represented its people rather than the citizen being subservient to the government. The fight between citizen and government in America has from its inception been based on a "Don't Tread on Me" concept: people always fighting to remain independent and having the ability to control their own destinies. With the growth of government and the denigration of the American citizen's expectations of "oneself," we have allowed the subliminal messaging system of Hollywood, Vegas, and our government to lower our standards as a citizenship.

In order to continue, we must break down the system to better understand what it is that drives our media, Hollywood, Las Vegas, and Federal Government. I believe most of you were able to immediately answer this question, but for those still guessing, the answer is *MONEY!*

When the business of network programing began the producers found it difficult to excel because of the heavy moral restrictions applied by the extremely ethically oriented American citizens. The citizens at this time were disciplined within the walls of morality, thus disallowing, restricting, and condemning vulgar language, nudity, lawlessness, prejudice, or anything deemed reprehensible by their rules of scripture. Did atrocities exist within this era...you bet they did, but they were on a much lesser scale than what we see in today's society.

This restrictive environment was a major dilemma for the *advertising of corruption* in the media industry. Thus close to its inception the industry leaders knew that unless they could find inroads to break down the rigidness of America's consumer, they would be limited in their ability to sell products. Let's not forget the goal of all the people and organizations I named as the perpetrators of the *"set you up to fail"* clan that is at the end of their breaking down the moral fiber of our citizenship: a giant pot of gold!

Successful advertising agencies know that in order to sell products, they need to break down the psyche of the *potential buyer.* In order to do this they must know the buyers' weaknesses. If we turn back in time, examining when the media and advertising began to make tremendous gains within America, we must return to the 1960's and the familiar phrase used to describe the boomer's (reference to Americans born between the mid-1940's through 1960) mantra of *"Sex, Drugs and Rock and Roll"* defining their era.

This group of American citizens referred to as the *Boomers* were destined to change America in a way that would payoff big for them. If we analyze the term *"Sex, Drugs and Rock and Roll"* as defining this generation, we realize that the success of network broadcasting was based entirely upon this premise. They knew the Boomers' proclivities and willingness to do drugs, along with a revolution happening within the music industry. This produced a subliminal message within their lyrics of *Nakedness, Drugs and Sex* that would be the perfect mix to drastically change the culture of America's past.

If we analyze human existence through religious scripture, we know the commandments placed upon humans by God's word are specifically designed to protect us from ourselves regarding our weaknesses that are a part of being human. Earlier generations within our history were no doubt sinful, but they were far more prone to carrying their guilt and being remorseful because of the religious hold upon our nation. What drastically changed America is when the protesting began in the 1960s as a statement against the Vietnam War. In addition to the protesting of the Vietnam War the boomers began to show their willingness to do drugs in order to enhance their experience in what would become a crazed Rock and Roll culture. Thus, began a mixture of emotion and change destined to deliver a wrecking ball to the rigid culture of America's past!

But we have come a long way down a road threatening disaster. Nowadays the use of advertising, whether it is for the sale or promotion of a product, service, or political viewpoint is somewhat like "fake news" and the use of television within our homes has become nothing more than a marketing tool. The days of watching a movie without some sort of message from a special interest group are over. Whether you recognize it or not, we are under attack from a marketing frenzy of subliminal messaging to constantly entice us to discard our values and to slowly break down the nation's acceptance of these new cultural changes…all in the name of MONEY!

CHAPTER 4

ECONOMY OF SIN

I must admit in my effort to problem solve I find it extremely difficult to suggest solutions to helping parents keep from being anxious and having a clear mind while they try to harvest wholesome children in an unwholesome environment. Trying to raise mentally stable children while they are being exposed to corrupt television advertising, Hollywood movies, dysfunctional network programming, and finally video games displaying graphic violence is a tough task. My worry is whether the recent changes in America's culture, fueled by what is now referred to as a technological revolution, have driven us to a point of instability beyond repair. If we expect America to thrive we must find a way to cultivate a large percentage of our citizenship into wanting a much more stable existence, living among one another under a higher standard of morality.

Many of the problems we are experiencing today as a country evolve around the thing we call money. The dictionary's definition of the word *"Money"* **is a current medium of exchange in the form of coins or banknotes, coins and banknotes collectively.** We as a citizenship understand money as a form of payment we receive for the work we perform either from our hourly or full-time jobs, a service we offer, or something we create and sell. Our entire ability to provide *"things"* for ourselves and our families is based on what we receive in the payment of money for something we provide.

As a child I recall hearing the phrase *"Money is what makes the world go around."* If we think about the context of this phrase, it is 100% spot on! Everything we do in life, whether it is the request of a service, the food we buy, signing your children up for a sports team, going on vacation, or going to a movie requires the exchange of money! The problems civil societies generally face stem from what people are willing to do in order to obtain the *payment of money!*

This my fellow citizens is the dilemma we face: will we continue the dream of being a free nation protecting the sanity of our citizens in order to remain a stable force leading the world as *(Ronald Reagan once termed)* "The shining city on the hill," or will we be discussed in history as a nation lost to self-destruction due to the corruption of money? If we dissect what happens within these *shining cities on the hill,* we know that many of the things transpiring for the exchange of money are not conducive to maintaining a long-term healthy society. As a matter of fact, if we review what occurs within our cities, we see they are a microcosm of what we see advertised upon our television sets daily.

If we analyze *"Sin City"* (Las Vegas), we know the main premise of what it has to offer is legalized gambling, prostitution, glamorous and not-so-glamorous live performances, and show girls in revealing costumes. The list of goes on and on, and all of this is happens within beautiful hotels with lavish amenities. In many cases these hotels offer the finest of foods available free of charge as long as you gamble there. Many people around the world believe that if you haven't experienced Vegas it is something everyone should include on their bucket list. Amazingly enough, there are families taking their yearly vacation to *Sin City* because of their enticing offers for a *free or discounted* room and free food. These hotels make it easy for Mom and Dad to set the kids up at the hotel pool while the parents go do some innocent gambling.

Please don't misconstrue or feel I am making a negative judgment on families choosing Vegas for their vacation. My purpose for writing this book is to discuss mental health topics in order to shed light upon our lives, helping you to dissect the areas of your life in which you are... "set up to fail." It is my feeling the advertisers of evil have caused social and cultural changes by promoting dysfunction as normal, and the result has placed many of our citizens in a vulnerable position.

If we review the history of our country from its inception it has been a predominantly Judeo-Christian society in which both religions are based upon the commandments delivered by one God. These commandments taught the followers of both Judaism and Christianity to be moral, putting upon our hearts that if we knowingly broke the laws of God's commandments we had clearly sinned. The atonement for your sins was handled differently by each of the religious institutions, but the consistent message from all of them was the feeling of guilt and the need for repentance to relieve you of your burdens of offense.

This I believe is the inner battle facing our nation within every aspect of our daily lives. Our inner souls and expectations of who we are have been based on a moral society living by the rule of law. Many of us as children lived within a rigid environment designed to guide us, always making sure we were walking a straight line. If at any time we started to go astray by breaking the rules, there was always a parent or an outspoken adult nearby reminding us to feel the guilt of our action and letting us know the consequences of these actions if we continued on the same path..

Before we continue I will answer the question beginning to formulate within your minds...the answer is no, I am not attempting to blame the problems we face as a country on formerly being too rigid a society that was made to feel guilt by religion! My goal is to shed light on the confusion we have as a people at the present time, in order to open the dialogue on how we begin to navigate this great ship known as *America* to calmer waters. The one thing we should all agree upon is that there are many people within our society who are confused, angry, scared, and without direction.

In order for us to have a real conversation about the direction of America's future, it must start with the people we elect as our leaders, better known as our representative government. What has become critically damaging to the health and well-being of our country's overall attitude is that our lack of trust in our government has reached an all-time high. If the people we elect as our representatives continue to damage our trust, their lack of moral leadership will have very damaging results.

America has been so successful because our government has been thought of by the majority of its citizens to be a nation governed by the rule of law. What has transpired over the last several decades is that we have witnessed a government that seems to have lost its way. Because our government is corrupted by money doled out by lobbyists and others, despite our attempts to elect leadership representatives who are willing take a stand and root out or expose the corruption, the results have shown it will not take long before our newly elected representatives become one of the Washington *DC Boys* or *Girls*.

What generally occurs from a government proven to be corrupt is that its citizens begin to develop a skepticism and disbelief in the government and the country's future as a whole. When people see high officials in their government who are guilty of criminal actions with no consequences of their actions, many citizens begin to get a sense of hopelessness, believing the system of government is broken and that it's just a matter of time before that nation collapses. There are also those who feel empowered by government corruption, believing that if the government is corrupt they have an open door to break the law as well. Since the laws are nonfunctional and the lawmakers disregard them, there is no need for us to follow them. The final result from this lack of moral leadership is that a large part of the population becomes disillusioned and despairing, with no hope for their future. However, another segment of the people feel empowered and emboldened and begin to pursue a life of illegality. Another consequence that we have seen in many parts of the world is that when a corrupt government is not held accountable to the laws they create it becomes more powerful than its citizens and creates new laws that are favorable to their illegitimate actions.

As we continue to analyze the changes happening within our country, we begin to understand why the mental and emotional health of our nation is endangered. We see corruption in government going unpunished, television programming providing programs that stress dysfunction, and we are inundated by political rhetoric used to divide us into collective opposing voting bases; on top of all this are the sensationalizing media networks competing to bring news to us in the form of crises… this continuously promotes a feeling of doom and fear of the future.

My hope is to enlighten you and to help you to understand that the majority of the good and promising things happening within our nation are not reported. If we look at our population as a whole, remember that we have 320 million people in this country trying to live civilly every day. If we take a step back and realize that the 24-hour news networks are working continuously to find new stories, we can conclude that America is **not in a state of dysfunction.** We are actually an amazing nation filled with productive people, many of whom always find a way to be ethically successful regardless of the attacks they face by the ever-present watchdogs who are looking for ways to undermine our mental health. As a strong people we continue to prove the resilience of the American DNA every day and our ability to go on regardless of the disruption thrown our way!

CHAPTER 5

DRUGS IN AMERICA

In an earlier chapter we discussed how musicians have written lyrics and songs detailing America's problems through song. Since we know popular musicians are one of the groups most challenged by drug and alcohol addiction, in this chapter we will look at "Drugs in America" as one of our subjects.

I ask that you open your mind while you read this chapter, since we are going on a journey some may think is "conspiratorial." Please continue to read, allowing me to present my information in a logical manner. I believe you will find my points valid and will agree with my deduction: that drugs create a large part of the economy that is responsible for employing many people with high paying "jobs" at the expense of many American families.

It always starts for me with the same question: how can America be plagued with the problem of drugs flooding into our nation when we have a multitude of agencies with the ability to eliminate the drug source at its roots? We have an army of anti-drug government organizations: the CIA, FBI, Army, Navy, Marines, Coast Guard, Federal and State police, DEA, Homeland Security, Local Police, and more, plus many private groups.

If we apply logic to analyze America's drug epidemic, it makes us wonder how we can have all of these agencies in place but we have far too little success at stopping the catastrophic effect of drugs in America. When attacking problems my mind always works the same way in breaking things down: I start with the premise that "for every action there is a reaction." So using this process regarding the drug problem, I ask what is the *reaction* to the action when it comes to drugs? We started this chapter asking how can it be that all of those agencies combined have not had a more profound effect on reducing the inflow of drugs. The first thing that hit me was **Jobs!**

Let's not misconstrue my deduction…at least in reference to the law enforcement side, but on the political side intentions are not so clear. Let's remember that 65% of our representative government residing within Washington D.C. is comprised of lawyers! If we review the number of jobs created as the *"reaction to the action of drug)."* We have already mentioned the law enforcement part of the job equation but we need to examine others involved in fighting drug abuse.

We should start with the court system because once the police apprehend the criminal or addict, they are subject to examination possibly followed by conviction and thus must attend a court

proceeding. The defendant accused of a crime either hires an attorney or is appointed one by the state. Depending on the severity of their drug-related crime, they could be locked up in the local jail; their conviction involves prison guards, bonds people, a warden, door security allowing prisoners' families entry into the courtroom, judges, lawyers, counselors, bailiff, court reporter, parole officer…the list goes on and on!

It's a spiraling effect for the drug addict and his or her family, having a terrible effect on the health and well-being of the family in general. A multitude of families in our nation have been touched by losing their child, parent, spouse, or sibling – loved ones – to the effects of drugs. We have paid a heavy price on our mental health as a nation dealing with the burden of drugs within our society.

To continue the conversation, we must discuss the impact drugs have had on our cost of living along with our sense of well-being and our safety. We know that drugs in America are one of the leading causes of theft, burglary, and murder. Many American families harbor a concern or worry that a family member may become a victim of drugs in some way.

Much of what we've discussed so far has focused on the illegal drug industry and how it feeds American jobs, but we must also analyze the legal side of our drug epidemic. Many family members started the use of narcotics innocently by taking prescribed medication for pain from an injury. Years later their addiction to this drug may surface after numerous prescriptions from various doctors to support their dependency. Once the legal addict can no longer obtain drugs legally, 85% of them end up being victims of the illegal drug industry.

Upon researching this issue what bothers me more than anything else is that the more addictive drugs are far easier to get than the less addictive ones such as amphetamines. Another curious fact is that drugs that are sedative in nature are easily obtained but those causing clients to be potentially more alert are extremely difficult to obtain because of federal restrictions reducing the ability to game the system. This system is similar to that for the availability of narcotics.

If we go through the same exercise with legal drugs as we did with illegal drugs regarding the job creation process, we know the legal side contributes to jobs such as doctors, nurses, psychiatrists, counselors, pharmacists, and others.. We also know that there are giant corporations that we call *big pharma* that develop and approve new drugs and that are responsible for employing millions of people around the world and particularly in this country.

Because this book is a discussion about our mental health as a nation, I would like to again apply my logic of the *"action/reaction"* thought process, focusing our thoughts on the ailment/treatment side of the pharmaceutical industry. I refer to this part of the drug industry as the *"treat but don't cure."* In this *"treat but don't cure"* part of the doctor's diagnosis (a home run for Big Pharma), the pay-off comes when physicians prescribe medications to be used for the remainder of a patient's life!

The jobs created for this *treat but don't cure* drug industry are the FDA (Food and Drug Administration), Scientists, Academic Professors, Medical Schools, Physicians, Medical Students, Drug Manufacturers, equipment makers, and more. Although it is not my intention to denigrate the work of science or the medical field, I believe as citizens that we should be better educated about how the system works and what its consequences are for you and your mental (and physical) health.

To start from the beginning (again attempting to stay away from conspiracy theory), I believe we should start with a well-known fact that the formation of medical science in America made huge gains when oil tycoon turned philanthropist John D. Rockefeller formed and funded the Rockefeller Foundation. Through his philanthropy his foundation was responsible for creating and funding the **Harvard School of Public Health, John Hopkins School of Public Health, London School of Hygiene,** and **Kaiser Wilhelm Institute for Brain Research.** Additionally, the Rockefeller Foundation provided funding to build Harvard Medical School, the University of Chicago, and several other medical schools. While John D was alive many gains in medical science were made; thus the family continued to fund the medical industry through his Foundation.

It is well known that Washington D.C. has become littered with lobbyists from the pharmaceutical industry coercing and paying off our politicians for more favorable laws regarding the distribution and creation of new drugs. We also know that like the Rockefeller Foundation *Big Pharma* is responsible for financing the salaries of many of the scientists responsible for creating drugs that work hand in hand with the *treat but don't cure* industry. I will not go any further into this area of questioning the validity of the pharmaceutical science and who is funding it, but I ask all Americans to be aware that the pharmaceutical industry is one of America's leading industries of enormous wealth. Has their design become one that merely creates drugs to treat ailments and not to cure them? Or has our medical school system become one that teaches a curriculum to students emphasizing which drugs to use for a *"treat but don't cure"* system, all for the sake of selling drugs? If we allow this to continue for the sake of enhancing and ensuring a corporation's profit, the drug industry is sacrificing human lives in an unending effort to increase their already soaring profits.

As we go on I will continue to demonstrate that our country's dependency on the drug industry and its catastrophic effects on us as a nation are part of the stress we feel in the current American way of life. It is my contention that much of this stress is intentionally placed upon us to keep us off balance, divided, depressed, and in a state of confusion so we will not become aware of their damaging practices. Many people who have become addicted to drugs as a result of a physical injury also remain on the drug because of its calming effects and reduction of emotional stress and depression.

Our nation's politicians have been speaking about the drug or opioid epidemic in America since George H. Bush's presidency. They actively ran the (Dare) program back in the 1980's using the "just say no to drugs" slogan. Yet the industry is still responsible for the many deaths from drug overdoses in our young and old alike. I hope to convince you by the end of our journey that the answer to treating a child's depression or his or her difficulties in the adolescent period is not solved by allowing a doctor to prescribe your child anti-anxiety or anti-depressant medications. The solution to helping your children is spending time with them learning their strengths and weaknesses and helping them overcome their problems and difficulties as they are happening. We cannot continue to allow drug corporations to provide mind-numbing drugs to sedate the feelings we or our children experience throughout our lives. It is our job as parents to help our children understand and confront the setbacks and gains in their daily lives. Guiding our children's mental health and well-being will help them to be productive, happy, and responsible adults.

CHAPTER 6

ANXIETY

Many of us have heard the term *"Money is the root of all evil."* After reviewing much of what I've described in previous chapters it looks like this coined phrase has meaning for us. I think it is best not to demonize the *thought of money* as the source of evil but rather the thought of what some people are willing to do to *obtain* money. We have many good citizens around the world who have created ideas benefiting humankind and have made a lot of money as a result. What has damaged our nation and caused a severe case of anxiety is the overabundance of subliminal messaging with the constant pursuit of selling *"an experience."*

In this chapter I would like to get back to the basics of human existence in order to discuss anxiety. I mentioned earlier that many of the children in Hollywood are being raised with the help of a family psychologist or psychiatrist as part of their daily lives. Normalcy for these kids and their doctors consists of squashing any sense of nervousness, runaway thoughts, feelings of confusion, hurt, or despair with *mind-numbing* or *mind-altering* drugs.

Unfortunately, many families have become victims of the philosophy of taking a pill as the solution to any physical or mental ailment they may have. This process of doctoring our pain and emotions has become a way of life for many American families. We have become programmed as parents to accept *doctoring* as an ongoing part of our children's lives. My intent is not to convince you one way or another on how much doctoring you need within your family's life but to help draw your attention to how much they are involved already. My goal is to discuss the mental health of us as citizens and to clarify why it is we are struggling with anxiety.

Doctoring starts within the first few days of a child's life but it is accompanied by the guilt and/or stress that begins in a parent's life when this *doctoring* begins. Such doctoring must start with a parent's choice or a parent's **emotion** regarding the subject of immunization. I do not wish to get into the discussion of determining who is right and who is wrong regarding this subject, since the scientific results are not finalized. However, I feel that the anxiousness created from the unknown is another element contributing to the anxiety of the American family.

We should keep in mind not long ago people involved in the medical industry were referred to as practicing medicine (*"he or she is a practicing doctor"*). It is not a stretch to say, that much of the evolution within the medical industry is *practice* and similar to the lab rat in the scientist's laboratory, we are also the *lab rats* of the medical industries' practice. It is important for us to have this discussion, as I feel the anxiousness created from the unknown…is another element within the anxiety of the American family.

Let's review the anxiousness parents experience within the first few days of their child's birth. The following are shots recommended by the CDC within the first year of an infant's life: **Hepatitis-B, Rotavirus, Diphtheria, Influenza Type B, Pneumococcal conjugate, Inactivated Polio IPV, Measles-Mumps-Rubella, Varicella, Hepatitis A, and Meningococcal Meningitis.** The controversy surrounding the argument regarding the quantity and the effects immunizations are having on newborn children is not a secret. Many parents are fighting legal battles with the claim that their child was completely normal (notably Jenny McCarthy and Jim Carey) before receiving these immunizations and after the shots numerous negative effects occurred.

If we get back to the subject of technology, we know that almost every family in America now has access to medical information; therefore when it comes to childhood immunization shots, there is plenty of information for a parent to research. Similar to our political parties and other areas, the medical industry has two parties, those for and those opposed to the immunization of children. When researching the available information, it doesn't matter which side a parent falls on; if they are for immunization, they accept the risk that something could go drastically wrong if their child has a negative reaction, or if they elect not to immunize they have the worry that their child is at risk for a list of diseases.

If we go a step further analyzing the stress a newlywed couple goes through during the first years of marriage understanding how the amount of change they experience can exasperate their stress. Their changing life might include the birth of child or (paying rent or a mortgage) for their first time. Additionally, many are just getting underway with their new career and are unclear of their earning potential. Some might enter the first few years of marriage carrying school debt and the thought of starting a family is overwhelming. So when these young families see and experience for the first time the love of a newborn child and feel the impact of responsibility, it is a completely normal reaction to have anxiety regarding all these new found experiences.

As we continue, I would like to quote an important phrase delivered from an American president at a pivotal time in America's history. During this era, America was suffering great hardship, and there was much confusion and fear as to the future of our nation. At this time, Franklin D.

Roosevelt delivered a speech at his inaugural address letting the citizens of America know: "*The Only Thing We Have to Fear Is Fear Itself.*" If I could give every American one piece of advice regarding any difficult situation…these words of wisdom can help carry you through your strife.

I will share with you a little bit about myself in order to be an example of what can be accomplished through this phase of life. As a child I was terribly shy regarding any situation that required me to be the center of attention. While attending school I would go as far as lowering my head in class to ensure that a teacher would not call on me name to answer a question! I viewed this shyness as a curse or disease because of the paralyzing effect it had. Unless you have had such shyness, you cannot begin to appreciate the effects it has on the person experiencing it..

For those who lack compassion or do not understand the subject of shyness, I ask you to think back to the first time you were asked to stand in front of the class and give your first speech in a classroom full of students! Although probably 1% of the population reflects upon their first experience with glee, the other 99% remember the nervousness that accompanied doing this. The problem for a person who is shy is the fact that this trait never really goes away and plays out over and over in any and every new experience he or she encounter. In my case although shyness might have impacted me in a classroom environment, I was lucky enough to have excelled in sports so there were areas of my life that did bring satisfaction. Whatever sport I played I was generally the quiet star of the team with a fierce drive not to beat the competition but to demand the most of my own ability. What sports taught me that school could not was the value of the *Team.* So many people today suffer because they feel they are traveling through life's problems alone, especially the folks who are riddled with *shyness*. I will explain in depth something I've learned in my 30years of business ownership managing people. I thank God every day that early on in my life someone saw a special quality within me they felt was worth promoting to lead or manage others. It may have been my seriousness or perhaps my approach to working with others and my willingness to help others who were struggling under pressure situations. For some reason my shyness did not hinder my performance under highly visible or pressure filled situations. What helped me make great strides as an adult with shyness was once I was put in a management position and responsible for building a team in order to help a business run effectively, I found my gift was seeing and understanding the signs and signals sent by the people that worked for me. It wasn't until I started working with others and listening to their problems that I was able to recognize that they had difficulties as well and I was not alone; everyone has hang-ups. For me to hear the problems of others were comforting and a relief to know I was not alone with my struggles and the anxiety associated with them. The only difference between me and some of those sharing their problems with me was because of my work ethic and drive to achieve, the shyness did not prevent me from reaching my goals.

For those fortunate enough to not struggle with these traits and who believe it is a sign of weakness to discuss life's struggles, I quote the expression of Jesus addressing the crowd that was getting ready to stone the prostitute: *"let he who is without sin... cast the first stone."* I say to those struggling to admit or not willing to discuss their weaknesses or shunning those who do...***strength is defined by a person willing to listen, having compassion, willing to help others who may struggle, never using another person's known weakness against them in order to empower oneself.***

What I hope to gain by focusing our attention on America's mental health is first and foremost to bring light to those struggling...and to help you understand you are not alone! Every person we know struggles with something; even if we can hide them we all have issues of concern.

Additionally, I hope I've made it clear that it is not by accident that we are seeing marriage and family problems and dysfunction on the rise. It is not by accident that the standards of our American families have far fewer expectations or goals than previously and that many of our citizens have become directionless, filled with anxiety, and feeling they are living a life empty of happiness.

As citizens and as individuals we must regain the strength of our convictions and begin to decipher what is causing us to alter our path. If we don't recognize and overcome our weaknesses they can lead us into a life of dissatisfaction or self-destruction. One critical element to living a happy, successful life is having the ability to self-reflect and own what you know to be your internal weaknesses. First and foremost, we must be willing to recognize and admit our weaknesses in order to learn how we can master the ability to fight the power of their distraction, thereby giving us the ability to live a happy and productive life.

CHAPTER 7

Do You Control Your Mind, or Does Your Mind Control You?

W hat a simple yet complex question "Do you control your mind, or does your mind control you"? The advertisers we've spoken of throughout the beginning chapters of this book believe that the general public has very little discipline and little to no control over their own minds or impulses.

Let's renew our discussion by reviewing human weaknesses such as addiction. I would like to be clear...I do not believe people with addictions *of any kind* are weak, but I think it is important to point out that the advertisers selling products or services believe that we as humans have tendencies to over-react to our weaknesses and that we inherently have little capability to overcome or stop the urge to react. They spend millions of dollars studying *personality/character* traits of social behavior, all in the name of penetrating and capturing a marketplace to sell their product!

Americans are spending countless dollars on seeing psychiatrists to help them solve their problems. Professional psychiatrists spend time analyzing each of their clients individually, generally starting with their childhood. They generally follow with adolescence to determine whether or not the problems started with a childhood dilemma or sometime later in life. Typically, once the psychiatrist finds something he or she feels is significant, the focus is on how these findings may have impacted you from the time they occurred and how they impacted your decision-making process from that point on. Helping the patient decipher or understand how an occurrence during childhood may have been internalized gives the psychiatrist a basis for finding the client's path to unhappiness or possibly self-destruction.

If we can accept the psychiatrist's idea that the messages we received during adolescence from our parents, siblings, and teachers are a precursor to our unhappiness or anxiety, then we can most assuredly accept the premise that the messaging we are receiving from our network programming and advertisements delivered through the media can also cause us to alter our behavior and has the potential to create obsessiveness, unhappiness, and anxiety on a massive scale!

Throughout life…I have always found success when I tried to simplify the things I wanted to learn or I struggled with due to my known weaknesses. In a later chapter I will relate that when I was 11 years old my parents divorced. I had many hang-ups and setbacks from the scars of divorce; no child is left without a scar. Many children who have gone through this experience might have heard parents yelling obscenities at one another or even at the child. Some suffered from having a parent abandon them, leaving the remaining parent in a state of distress and sometimes causing them to use drugs or alcohol in order to cope. What we know for certain is how we allow messaging to alter the way we think or act. Do you control your brain, or does your brain control you?"

Scientific research tells us our brain functions and thought processes are what cause the human species to excel over any other living species. We have the ability to compute, engineer, have feelings of emotion, calculate strategy -- the list of things we do as humans is endless. Some people can be extremely focused and as a result they have the ability to accomplish amazing things. Others who lack the ability to focus may have trouble getting started on their desires because they are stifled by indecision caused by fear or distractions. The same excuse is often heard: "I started… but was not able to finish because more important things came up." Does this sound familiar?

The cause of distractions could stem from predetermined messaging formulated from childhood trauma or the constant barrage of subliminal messaging we receive as adults in our daily lives. It may be as simple as you were watching a television reality show, sitcom, or cable news that may have caused a distraction, triggering your messaging system that was wired from an experience during childhood or an experience suffered as an adult.

In order for us to control our brain it is necessary to understand what is transpiring within our messaging system in our brain. What I mean is we need to understand our messaging system and learn how our predetermined response mechanism reacts to certain occurrences and feelings such as crisis, joy, pride, guilt, fear, and so forth.

We must start with the premise that our brain is our own, and it will not be controlled or dictated to through someone else's messaging that is attempting to hijack our response mechanism to occurrences in order to sell a product or take advantage of us in some other way.. The response mechanisms I am referring to within your messaging system start with two key factors…the first is *panic* and the second is the *emotional* or *impulse* response. I believe by identifying and learning to control these two responses we can control our brain and not allow its reaction to control you.

The important thing to understand is that reactions can be changed if we logically identify how we react to something emotionally; it does not require going back to our childhood or putting you on medication in order to change these predetermined reactions. I believe reactions are learned and do not have to remain with you forever.

It simply requires the power of understanding your predetermined response and then deciding that you and you alone control this messaging and not some outside force!

As I mentioned my goal is to keep things simple and in order to control my brain I found the key element was to identify my initial response to an occurrence. People carrying a trait that stems from shyness generally have an immediate response when put in a position where they are visible to the public; this causes their messaging system to react with panic. Because the first impulse of reaction is panic, it triggers the shy person's messaging system to respond to the panic with emotion, basically causing them to go into a shell saying "I don't want to be here!" Once they reach that stage as an emotional response, it is no longer you controlling your brain but your brain's response mechanism controlling you.

I am not making light of the power of these response mechanisms, but it is critical to understand that the message of panic we receive when entering into an environment outside our comfort zone is nothing more than thoughts. My contention is if you can have the thought to panic and lose control, you can also have the thought to control the panic once you feel it start to set in. For people suffering with the trait of shyness..." *panic messaging*" immediately starts once they get outside their comfort zone, feeling people can visually see they are not comfortable, thus causing the emotion of panic and the feeling of losing control.

There are psychiatric drugs, and a plethora of books that make a great deal of money treating the reaction response to what I refer to as triggered messaging. People are spending countless hours and dollars researching what might have happened to them in their early life that is causing them to be mired in emotional turmoil. I believe we can take a step back and simply identify our response mechanism to different life occurrences, and by doing this we will be better able to understand ourselves and the directions we chose in our daily lives.

When discussing panic or emotional response, I like to use the example of giving a speech because most people can remember a time in their lives when they learned their response mechanism to this event. To those of you who were or are presently paralyzed with fear at the thought of standing in front of a group of your peers giving a speech, you should take comfort in knowing that 90 percent of those people you are speaking to are glad it's you up there and not them! My main reason for sharing that truth is that we all have this inherent tendency to abuse ourselves by thinking it is only us who suffer from this horrible feeling, whereas in all actuality most of your peers feel the same way.

Taking that statement, a step further...I believe most of the problems/emotions we suffer with as a people are actually shared by that same 90 percent I mentioned earlier. Where things go bad for some of us is when we become reclusive with our thoughts, allowing our panic to become a bludgeoning hammer telling our messaging system that we are weak and unable to cope. It is at this time that people begin to unravel and find it difficult to cope with even the simplest of life's problems; this prompts them to seek help.

Again...let me be clear. I am not making light of the emotional state some of you are finding yourselves in. It is a terrible feeling to be alone with a sense of being unable to cope. My message to you is *you are not alone!* As I write this book, I take great pleasure in sharing my thoughts and using them as therapy to solve my own problems. I also take comfort in knowing there are others out there like me who are not perfect. I believe understanding that we are all human and that none of us is perfect is the key to relieving unreal expectations of oneself. Once we remove the expectations and self-degradation, we can learn who we are and attempt to figure out our comfort zone within society.

Later we will discuss identifying common personality traits and their responses, along with a few exercises to help us know who we are as individuals and how we can better cope with life's challenges. There are two things I would like you to gain from this chapter: the first is you are not alone with the things you feel because the messaging we receive from the onslaught of media programming is consistent to all of us. The second thing I hope you've learned is that our responses to daily occurrences are thoughts that have been conditioned by the way we have reacted to something in the past. If we understand the concept that our brain and its thoughts should be controlled by you and not that your brain is a separate entity independent of your body's deciding how you will react to daily occurrences, you will then be on a clearer path to finding happiness that works within the comfort zone you choose!

CHAPTER 8

THE ONLY THING WE HAVE
TO FEAR IS FEAR ITSELF!

I will start by speaking to all the ill-informed people out there who may attempt to apply the title of this chapter to things such as jumping off cliffs or doing 150-mph on a motorcycle...that is not the intent of this phrase!!! If we go back to the time in America's history when FDR used this historical statement, it is crucial for us to realize he was speaking to an American people who had lost hope in America as the land of opportunity. What is not discussed is what FDR said prior to this iconic phrase which is, "This great Nation will endure as it has endured, and will revive and prosper."

Many of the older readers might be slightly more familiar than some of the younger folks with the story of Franklin D. Roosevelt. In order to understand the purpose behind his statements we must quickly reflect on the time of his presidency. Please stay with me, I promise I am not veering off into a world of politics.

In 1921 FDR at the age of 39 became ill with an autoimmune disease that would ultimately leave him paralyzed from the waist down. What many people didn't know and at the time and the media didn't cover it, being paralyzed from the waist down meant that his bodily functions didn't perform like a normal person's. One can only imagine the challenges this man faced on a daily basis and the strength it took just to deal with his illness.

If we reflect on FDR's presidency, he became president of the United States in 1932, which is considered one of the lowest points in our nation's history. His election in 1932 was the people's choice to help America regain its strength from the greatest known depression to hit any westernized civilization lasting from 1929 until 1939. Much of the economic welfare programs we have today began during FDR's presidency due to the catastrophic conditions and hardships citizens faced at this time.

What I would like to discuss is what was it about this man that gave him the strength to guide us through *The Great Depression, World War Two,* and ultimately to be the only person to have served three terms as president of the United States. What was it that drove FDR to these accomplishments? Let's take it one step further by analyzing America and its people, dissecting what it is about the American DNA that drives us to overcome adversity.

I've dedicated much of my business career to managing many different segments of the American people. My greatest joy in life other than my family has been helping all levels of citizens achieve their goals within a style that works for them and *not a one style fits all method.* I often use the analogy that God gives every person something that comes easily to them *(a gift).* The *gift* I received from God is the ability to help others find, understand, and excel with their gifts.

When training new employees at their job, I explain the goal or task we're trying to achieve and then help them achieve that *goal or task* in a manner best fitting their style of achievement. Unless it is a production line with specific procedures, in most cases it does not matter how one gets to the end goal, as long as each person can produce results achieving the same outcome. My success in business has been allowing people within the organization to be individuals owning their jobs in a way that best suits their style. By using this process, it has helped me maintain long-term employees and long-term success.

What I've found to be consistent with the American people is an independent spirit and *a will* to keep fighting regardless of the conditions. There are some employees who are exceptions to the rule, but I've found that even the people with poor attitudes, if inspired correctly, can be changed by helping them find their *gift* and giving them a chance to succeed as an individual. This independent spirit and will to succeed always shine through! My goal is for each of you to understand and be proud of your American DNA, and to help you find your gift. After discovering your gift, hopefully you will be able to create a business or find a job that allows you to excel in a manner that comes easily to you.

It is my contention that the new immigrants joining us every day are the prime examples of what I refer to as the formation of this American DNA. To put it simply, most immigrants coming to America have left their existing homelands in order to flee oppression. The common element our ancestors have with these newcomers is similar to the plight of our families in that they had the guts to flee their original place of origin, often leaving behind their families, their belongings, or even their culture—risking everything to join the *land of the free*!

My concern for American families who had ancestors arriving many years ago is that much of the independent spirit and work ethic required to exist in those difficult times may have dissipated within many of our families. We have been gifted by generations of sweat from our ancestors who have built an infrastructure that offers help to those in need, and eliminated the fear of starvation. The question we must reflect upon is, have we become a people who have lost the value or the importance of the constant need to replenish an infrastructure built by a strong work ethic and independent spirit? These values must be retaught within our homes and our educational system, always emphasizing the plight of our courageous ancestors and their journey to become a free people. Whether you are a new citizen or your ancestors came to this country many years ago, it is every American's responsibility to teach their children that our freedom was not given to our forefathers, *they fought and died for it!*

Much of our present complacency comes from many of the things we've discussed in prior chapters. During the era of FDR, times in America were so dire it that it required our nation to create help for citizens who had lost everything. The attitude of the people in this time period was a thankfulness that the government offered help, but there was no shame or guilt in the reception of it. For many of those receiving government assistance (also referred to as *relief*), because of their positive spirit they did all they could to get back on their feet as quickly as possible. They were also sure to try to replenish the system that provided them with help in their time of need.

In order to explain the formation of this independent spirit of American DNA, I believe it is best to compare our country to a family business that has been handed down through generations. The stories always begin in the same way, usually starting with a great-great-great grandparent having come to America with nothing more than the clothes on his or her back and five dollars in their pocket! The plight of these courageous newcomers usually started with a business begun in a one-room shack or with a family member peddling goods in a cart on a city street built by hand in their one-room home. However the business may have begun, what they had in common was that they all started with a dream of some family member driven to be independent and self-reliant.

What we understand about the American way of life back then is that these families who were helping to build our nation had no alternative but to live frugally. During America's formative years, the goal was to build an infrastructure within our nation for the purpose of creating stability for their families and the generations of American families to come. These people were resilient and disciplined and taught their children the value of a strong work ethic. They explained the necessity of being productive in order to preserve what they accomplished, knowing how easy it was to lose their gains. These folks came here with nothing but the shirts on their backs and modern-day things such as *unemployment, food stamps, subsidized housing, Social Security,* and *Medicare* did not exist. If they were not self-reliant, caring for themselves, they knew there was little to no help available.

Many of these early settlers whether they came from the farms of Europe, or were peddlers from the city streets so they were understood the importance of cultivating the soil in order to produce new crops each year. Many of them used their principles of cultivation (or logic) and applied them to a way of life. To express what I mean, let's use an example picturing a rose garden to represent our children and a fruit tree to represent our country. I believe that this simple logic built on sound principles and timeless practices can still be used in building our family values today.

The ancestors we speak of would be thought of as *simple* people in today's America, but this age-old cultivation of the soil, reaping and preserving the harvest used by these early settlers, taught their families how to grow their businesses by explaining that the importance of preparing the soil (or foundation) was paramount to the success of farming or business. They used the logic of farming to raise their families, thinking of their children's foundation (manners, work ethic) in the same manner as they did preparing the soil. Because many of them were farmers, they thought of their children as a rose within a garden and knew the necessity to pull the weeds in order for the flower to flourish and bloom.

They taught their children the value of a strong work ethic and the importance of making good decisions, always with the intent of producing crops or products for their families and their country, being sure to keep the weeds of life from destroying their rose garden *(children)*. They taught farming principles that when weather conditions were conducive to producing a plentiful supply of crops, it was critically important to be prepared *"To make hay while the sun shines"* Additionally, because of the unpredictability of weather and its potential impact to farming they stressed the importance of *"Saving for a rainy day."*

Throughout this chapter I have compared America as a country to a family business, because it is important for us as citizens to understand our role as citizens in America is similar to our role in a family business. We have remained independent as a nation because our citizens understood the value of being independent and productive. The feeling of accomplishment and satisfaction we get from having a good job or business that supplies us with enough income to meet our daily financial needs and perhaps pay for our children's education should be something we are proud of!

In addition to being prudent within our personal lives and assuring we have enough income to meet our family's needs, as productive citizens we must also be proactive, making sure our government is accountable to the people by using our tax money wisely. We must have a government that keeps our nation secure from our enemies and ensures law and order in order to provide a stable infrastructure for our families. This gives us the chance to cultivate productive families for America's future. We should collectively make it our duty to teach our families why it's important to be productive in all aspects of our lives and do our part to contribute in keeping America safe. This will give us the assurance that we have *"saved for a rainy day."* As I mentioned earlier, I have owned a business and managed people most of my adult life. What has concerned me in recent years is that I am finding a number of America's younger generation and a large number of immigrants are not aware that the *federal and state* taxes deducted from their paychecks are used to pay the salaries of our elected government. Many of them are not aware that the politicians we see on television making promises for free stuff (such as free healthcare or a free education) *is from money taken from the taxpayer.* We as parents must make sure that our children understand that there is no such thing as a free ride and that the government can only provide benefits for them after they become taxpayers and productive citizens.

We must educate our children, helping them to understand that government officials who promise they will tax the wealthiest and redistribute these tax dollars to pay for their education are deceiving us and them. What the politicians neglect to disclose is that the wealthy own most of the stores or businesses supplying our goods and services that we pay for as consumers and they are simply passing on to you the consumer any and all tax increases they receive from the government by raising the price of those goods and services.

The basis of this discussion is still the *mental health of America.* As I mentioned in earlier chapters, we are being overwhelmed as a nation and kept off balance until some of us reach a state of despair. We must recognize that a battle is being waged for the independent soul of the American citizen. If we analyze the things we've discussed, such as the cultural changes happening within America, we can recognize that these changes are being directed by diversionary tactics and the use of subliminal messaging. We as a nation cannot be naïve, believing all of what has transpired has been occurred by coincidence.

When FDR created government programs, they were designed on the original principles of prudent planning and not taking more than the earth or *your country* can provide. As our president, he understood that the American DNA was built from a principled work ethic, and he knew that the families within American society were teaching their children the value of being productive and to be prudent with their money on a long-term basis in order to *"save for that rainy day."*

What we are seeing throughout America is a new culture of people who are no longer saving for a rainy day. They are living from paycheck to paycheck hoping bad weather never comes! Many families are teaching new generations of children how not to work, educating them as to how to play the system in order to depend on the federal government to provide them with a free ride. These are the people who no longer understand the value of a working life and the self-satisfaction it brings, allowing us to maintain the independent spirit of our American DNA.

The decline of a work ethic in America is the greatest burden placed upon the backs of the next generation and will require discipline and strength to change the entitlement culture that has developed within American society. When FDR spoke to a nation explaining *"The only thing we have to fear is fear itself,"* he was speaking to a people that understood that they were responsible for themselves. The citizens of this era knew that the *relief* FDR offered was temporary and because of the catastrophic conditions and that the help he provided was designed to be temporary and to last just long enough to allow them to get back on their feet. I will make my case throughout this book regarding the importance of understanding and knowing that we as a people should expect nothing more than what we have earned and saved individually. This country and the bloodlines of our American DNA was created by a people made of grit and determination; there was no challenge too great! When FDR delivered his words of wisdom, our nation eventually forged ahead to build bridges and skyscrapers within our cities like nowhere else in the world!

In order to defeat these current challenges, we must approach them in the same manner our ancestors did. They cultivated this nation through toughness and hard work and the attitude that all citizens must do their part. They did this independently and yet collectively together, inspiring and challenging one another to achieve great outcomes. I believe that this DNA still resides within us and that we will prove to the world that there is yet another generation of Americans ready to take on new challenges and proving that a free people guiding a free nation can work!

CHAPTER 9

WHO ARE YOU?

N ow that we have discussed a little bit of history and the plight of a nation built by extremely tough circumstances, let's return to our current era and discover *who we are* and how we can advance as a strong and confident people helping to guide our families and our country in a positive direction.

The difference we face today versus the time of FDR is that America is no longer a place where the primary goal is to build an infrastructure of productive families. It has unfortunately become a massive flea market for venders to sell products! What we must do as citizens is decide where we fit within this new America and how we can fight the distractions it brings to us and our families' *mental health.* The course of technology within America is set…it is up to us to decide whether we will allow the onslaught of mass media messaging to control our minds and our impulses. The opposite course is do we as a nation want to send a message to the advertisers telling them "we are controlling our minds and not your subliminal messaging seeking to entice impulse!"

The challenge we face to regain our mental health should not be taken lightly. There is messaging in our music, television programs, movie theaters, educational systems, billboard signs … everywhere. So as we attempt to regain our *mental health* we must start from the ground up seeking to build a foundation for each of our strongest individual traits. As I share these thoughts with you, I hope that each person reading this book will internalize the thoughts unique to his or her individual DNA/personality traits. As I mentioned earlier, I discovered through management that allowing each person their individuality and helping them find a way to be successful in his or her own way is the key to success.

I've mentioned several times throughout this book that each and every one of us is born with an individual gift...something that comes naturally to us in our own unique way. The challenge is to discover this unique gift and gear the things we do in our daily lives to utilize it as much as possible.

Earlier I mentioned that my gift is having the ability to see other people's gifts, and along with this I've been given the motivation to help others excel with their gifts. The reason I believe this to be important is that the more things we can accomplish within the realm of our *gift*, the more comfortable we feel in our environment and are less susceptible to panic and anxiety. My goal is for each of us to exist with as few of the ongoing stressors as possible. If we have the knowledge that we can better cope with the sensation of feeling overwhelmed, we will be better prepared at keeping our stressors from spinning out of control.

To give you an example: I have found that the employees within our organization who are more introverted or shy actually seem to perform better in a crowd! By putting them into the proper setting and letting them work within their comfort zone, they can be some of the most productive people, and the good thing is you don't have to reprimand them for talking too much!

Let's get started helping you find your *gift*, empowering you to communicate with your friends, family, and business acquaintances, ultimately strengthening how you function, and giving you the tools to participate better with others. In order to find *"who we are"* it will require us to make a list of our known strengths and our known weaknesses. I realize his is an age-old strategy, but when compiling this list I would like you to do this a little differently than the standard strength and weakness list typically done in psychology class. We're going to approach this differently by helping you to learn how to understand yourself better by finding what I call your comfort zone. To start this process we're going to retitle the strength and weakness list and refer to it as a *comfort/ non-comfort* list.

In order to complete this *comfort/non-comfort* list, I would like you to focus your thoughts on things that knowingly bring you comfort or said another way, things that settle your nerves. This list can include anything: it might be spending time with your family, being home alone, going for a walk, visiting your parents, sharing thoughts with your spouse or a friend, doing favorite parts of your job, playing or watching your favorite sport, or doing hobbies you like and how you feel while doing these "comforts.". The items on this list should exclude any tasks or actions that producer stress or anxiety in any way. Our goal is to shine a light on the things that bring you happiness.

Once you've completed the *comfort* list, it's time to make another list of the things that take you out of your comfort zone. This we refer to as the *non-comfort* list, and it should include the things that knowingly give you anxiety. This list can include situations you find uncomfortable at work, bothersome things you deal with at home, topics of discussion you find uncomfortable, interacting with people you don't like and the reason you do not like them, things that bother you about your parents or siblings, daily tasks you dislike, and so forth.

This non-comfort list is not one we will be sharing with others, so it's important to be honest in order to truly understand the things that make you anxious and it is also important to find what brings you comfort. Remember the purpose for doing this is to help us find *"who we are,"* by helping us find the things that bring us joy and identifying the things that bring us negativity. I believe once we identify the *thoughts* that either alleviate or add stress we can help you discover ways to empower the *comfort* thoughts and to reduce the negative feelings associated with the *non-comfort* things in your daily existence.

The key concept in the last paragraph that helps is to control our brain and not allow our brain to control us and to understand that these comfort and non-comfort feelings we have represent the way we think and internalize these stressors and nonstressors. Once you've completed the *comfort and non-comfort* list, this gives us the power to analyze our trigger points so we can start to change the way we think and internalize our thoughts. By doing this it gives us the ability to decide if we want to change the way we think about certain things bothering us or if we want to try to eliminate them from our lives. The critical thing to understand is that you must control your *thoughts* and understand the basis of those *thoughts,* thus giving you the ability to change the way you think about them.

Let me explain the concept of *"thought"* a little further. Let's remember that doctors and pharmaceutical companies are making huge sums of money on the premise that you have uncontrollable personality traits that limit you to the restrictions living within you. Their solution to solving the problem is providing therapy or medication in order to help you cope with what they refer to as inherent personality traits. So the concept that the problems you have are merely *thoughts* and that you have the ability to change or control these *thoughts* goes up against a lot of our economic systems that are thriving from the unstable mental health of our nation.

Without taking this conversation into a conspiratorial direction, I ask you to think logically about what the medical industry has in place and at stake if people realize they are in control of their minds and *their minds* are not being controlled by subliminal messaging that creates negative impulse reactions. We should understand the reality of how much **is to be lost or gained** by corporations along with the medical industry if they were to lose the majority of our citizens living on the edge with *out of control thoughts* and believing there is no hope because they are wired by stimuli that cause them to react in an uncontrollable way.

Let's take this a step further and imagine the devastation to these industries if we were able to grasp the power of being disciplined and controlling our brains. Imagine if we as citizens were able to identify the comfort and non-comfort things transpiring within our daily lives, and we had the ability to simply turn anxiety on and off as if it was nothing more than a light switch. Imagine if the majority of people struggling with mental health issues could be taught to simply logically examine their thoughts with the understanding they are merely thoughts, and if you can think about them one way you can certainly think about them in another way!

Let's remember our fears as children when our parents put us to sleep and we lay in bed frightened of the dark because we were sure we saw someone in the room or closet. Our parents had to come in several times and to teach/prove to us that there was not a boogie man in the room.. How did we get over this fear? We believed our parents and we consciously accepted that it was our mind seeing things that weren't really there. It was at this time that we actually took control of our *thoughts*, stopping our brain from controlling us! We learned that the boogie man was something our mind created, and we learned how to control the fear by controlling the thought.

Every adult should have the confidence they need to solve mental setbacks in their lives by overcoming *fears* through thought control. It is possible that these fears have left us with scars, but if we reflect back and understand how we were able to alleviate the paralyzing portion of the original *fear/thought in the past,* then we can certainly remove the remaining remnant or scar by understanding it is nothing more than how we *thought* about something, and thoughts can be turned off just like lights. Like politics, science has labeled us as a predestined species living within the traits we inherit with a general premise that people are prewired to react in certain ways to stimuli. I do agree with the theory that each of us has inherited a genetic response mechanism, but I disagree with the idea that it cannot be controlled. My contention is that by simply understanding the comfort and non-comfort things you identify in your life and discovering *your gift* of things that come easily to you, you can simplify and put logic to your thoughts. The courage we have displayed throughout our lives has been achieved through our own subliminal messaging...unknowingly, we've used FDR's statement of "The only thing we have to fear is fear itself." This will help us overcome our battle with our negative thoughts. Each of you has decided within some part of your life to overcome fear, understanding that the fear of not accomplishing the challenge was far worse than the act of doing it. In many instances you have been successful in many situations throughout your life, overcoming tremendous hurdles, so now it is time to reflect on the remnants of those hurdles and clean up the mess they left behind.

In order to start the next process, it is time to discover your gift! To do this we will need to make another list similar to the one we created for the comfort/non-comfort breakdown. This time you are going to make a list of the things you do in your daily life that can be done with little effort (meaning you do not struggle). This list should include tasks, hobbies, responsibilities at work, and so on and should be done in the same way we approached the *comfort, non-comfort* list. The difference is that we don't have to like or dislike the things we put on this list; we are merely searching to identify what they are. My point is that even though you may not like something that seems to come easily to you, it is good for us to identify what it is so we can tweak it to be an advantage.

Just to help get you started I will share a few thoughts about myself. As I mentioned, sports came easily to me and although I was pretty good at all of them, I particularly excelled at playing baseball. When I was a kid we didn't have many indoor things to do, so growing up in the Midwest as a young boy at 10years of age I would brush off my baseball mitt and cleats in the spring, and my brother and I would start playing catch early in the month of March. It was still brutally cold at this time, but signs of spring were on their way and the ice we had been skating on during the winter had melted.

Once April came around it was still cold and rainy, but it was time to call the kids down the street and start organizing games or get started on practicing skills. What I found is that I could never get enough of the game of baseball, so much so that even if my brother or a friend was too busy to throw me the ball, I would throw a superball at a garage door in order to continue working on my skills.

Not to get too long winded about me but to help you understand what I've learned about myself should help you to identify your *gift*. Baseball would start around mid-April continuing until the end of August, which meant in early September the transition would begin from the end of the baseball season to the beginning of football practice. I was a quarterback in football, which required a lot of practice because all of the plays were called by the coach on the sidelines with hand signals. So I had to learn the plays and memorize the hand signals, because if I screwed up one of the plays or didn't recognize one of the signals, I was in big trouble!

Football would continue until the end of November, and once completed the wait began for the weather to get cold enough for the lake to freeze for hockey and there was snowfall for sledding! My point for providing the sequencing of my childhood sports schedule is to explain that when making my list attempting to discover my *gift,* I reflected back on my childhood remembering that although I was involved in three different sports, whenever I had idle time I would use it to practice baseball. In other words, baseball was the sport that came naturally to me and the one I went to every time I had a free moment.

After analyzing my list, I realized that it was my experience from baseball that would later help me find my *gift* of managing people. Because I had excelled at baseball and also showed a willingness to help teammates be better at the sport, there were several times when my friends' parents would ask if I could come to their homes to help their son improve his baseball skills. This was a no brainer for me; I loved to help, and it was not work because of my love for the game!

The point of relating my story is to help you reflect back upon your childhood, helping you to recall fond memories of things you did and to attempt to understand their significance and how they impact you today. For instance, I was a skills guy and I had a natural inclination to help others, so it is not out of line that I became involved in owning and managing a team of people in the construction industry. I recall having friends who were more into baseball cards, memorizing the stats of each player and studying their cards in their spare time.. Comparably I had an interest in the players' stats but I found that I was more interested in studying the players' swings that were responsible for producing those stats. My point is that several of the guys collecting cards and reviewing stats were more inclined to do accounting jobs or data collection later in life rather than a skills type job.

Once you begin to realize what it was you enjoyed throughout your life, you can start analyzing your past and your career, reviewing whether any of the things you are presently involved in fit the things that came easily to you as a child. . However, because many of you (like me) may not have been afforded the opportunity to choose a career of choice, you must look within the career you do have, observing if there are jobs available within your chosen profession that align with your natural interests or skills. In other words, are you a data collector, are you a manager, do you like to write, or are you an organizer of information? Identifying the things that come naturally to you can help you find joy in all aspects of the things you do in life and in your career.

Conversely, as we discussed earlier learning the things we do not like to do helps us make better decisions on how we choose the path of our lives. As an example, I recall seeing a reporter interviewing several people having lived to 100 years of age. The interview that struck me the most was when the reporter asked a 100-year-old gentleman what was his secret to living a long, healthy life. The gentleman paused and then answered, *"I had a heart attack when I was 52 years old!"* The reporter was dumbfounded by his response and asked him to explain The man continued with his story, explaining after he had a heart attack he reanalyzed his life and his job and he decided to do only the things he found joy in and let others handle the things he didn't.

So essentially what this 100-year-old man did was analyze his *gifts* (things that came easily) and lived the remaining 48 years focusing on creating life conditions that removed negative energy that was causing him undo stress. I understand that it is not possible to remove everything we do not like from our lives, but it is possible to gear our lives toward the things we do like. If we can fill our lives with things that naturally fit our *gifts*…we can reduce the feeling of being *overwhelmed by panic* when we need to do the things we don't like. Additionally, if we understand more about ourselves, it will help us make better decisions in guiding the direction of our lives.

As we started this chapter I asked the question *"who are you?"* In a previous chapter I asked the question, *"do you control your brain or does your brain control you?"* We have discussed the concept that our *thoughts* do not have to be driven by emotional impulses responding to subliminal messaging. We have shown that throughout our lives each of us has the ability to complete tasks by using our *thoughts* to control our brain. . Each day we prioritize our *thoughts* deciding what we will accomplish for any given day. What this proves is that throughout our day we control our lives by handling normal daily functions. We are not confused or distracted when entering a dark room…we turn the light on! It is my contentions that once we understand that our subconscious is under attack from subliminal messaging, attempting to rule us through your impulses; we can eliminate our impulse reaction as though we are merely turning on and off a light switch.

If we think about this logically with the understanding that it is you who controls the thoughts happening within your mind, you will realize that it is up to you to be accountable for the decisions you make as individuals. If we understand this simple concept we can think ourselves into a life of happiness, realizing there is no end to using *thought* control to help us to find happiness in all aspects of what we do. It is time to learn *who you are* and control your destiny!

CHAPTER 10

FAMILY MATTERS

I f we are going to keep America safe, we must start by discussing our nation's most important element of strength: *"Family."* The term *family* has two meanings: the first is our family of genetic bloodline (e.g., mother, father, brother, sister, kids); the second is our family of fellow Americans. We cannot remain a strong nation, continuing our success as a people if our families are emotionally broken, so we must start with rebuilding the foundation of our families through good parenting.

As in the last chapter, I will attempt to use visualization as a way to describe effective parenting done a few different ways. As parents, we must do all we can to give our children a foundation that allows them to stand on firm ground, assuring them of the support they need during times of turbulence. A strong foundation is what helps our children navigate uncharted waters. Our goal is to provide them with enough strength and knowledge that will help them maintain their mental health as they face the multitude of distractions presented to them on a daily basis.

Because of the messaging we see through television programming and social media, the number of young people getting married and the success rate of marriages are at an all-time low. Much of this has to do with the messaging we receive that pounds us with the thought that there is a world out there that must be experienced, and so the idea of getting married and being committed to someone will destroy our chances to experience life. To be clear, I am not attempting to convince those of you who need to sow your wild oats to throw away your bucket list of adventures. I am however warning you that if your bucket list includes drugs and liquor, loose women or men, and hanging out in places that harbor illegal or immoral activities, it will leave you with experiences that stay with you for lifetime. Being born in 1960, I saw firsthand the results of the *sex, drugs, and Rock and Roll* representing the boomer culture. What we know now is a that a large percentage of those folks ended up with *Sexually Transmitted diseases, brain damage due to drug abuse and severe hearing loss from Rock and Roll!*

Unfortunately, once you choose the path of following such enticements, many times this path can destroy your life's future. It is my experience that finding the right person to share your life with is the one key essential element that can bring you joy on a long-term basis. If nurtured properly, this joy will last much longer than a thrill or experience. Finding the right person to share a lifetime commitment with is one of the most important decisions you will make in your life. You must be certain that you and the person you are choosing understand the commitment and both of you are willing to stick it out during tough times. I know the importance of this on a personal level because my parents divorced when I was 11. The damaging effects of being shifted to new schools and relocated from the home and neighborhood you grew up in can create tremendous damage and cause insecurities in a child's life.

When considering marriage, it's important to analyze and discuss with your potential partner their understanding of this commitment, making sure to address each other's expectations. Many of our religious institutions condemn divorce, labeling the divorcees as sinners and sometimes excommunicating them from their place of worship.. These are harsh terms and most of our religious institutions have backed off from this stance, but the reality of divorce and its lasting effects on your mental health will do great damage, especially if there are children. So choosing a partner who is committed to the long haul is essential to success.

What comes next…if you find the right partner and are lucky enough to receive the gift of a child (either through birth or adoption), there's no greater shared experience bestowed on the human species! There is no thrill ride or site-seeing cruise or Los Vegas experience comparable to the joy of having a child! The birth of a child allows you and your spouse to connect in a way that joins your DNA for life. The parents of a child conceived together are the only people on earth who can truly understand the delicate blueprint of their child's DNA. That is why it is critical for each of you to remain that child's parent, committed to shaping your child's mind and emotions, giving them specific input to build a sturdy foundation in order to help shape the stability needed to face life's challenges.

Let's go a step further with our discussion because there is much confusion and interaction within our child's life to the time he or she reaches adulthood. We as parents cannot fall victim to *believing or allowing* others to mismanage the receptors your child receives. It is my belief that engaged parents are the best resource to understanding how their child receives messaging. Therefore your involvement requires you to be sure that while your child is experiencing life's growing pains, you are there explaining the meaning of these experiences in a way that only you as the parent know how to so the child truly receives the value of the lesson.

I will continue to emphasize the importance of understanding our children. Because they have been built specifically from the DNA of both parents, collectively you will see signs from this child that only both of you can understand regarding what is transpiring within his or her mind. Additionally, if you communicate well within your marriage, you and your spouse can identify signs from your child that each of you see within each other. Being so much a part your child's life and knowing this information helps you to build a solid foundation for your child's growth.

We must realize the value of pulling weeds from our children early on, teaching them the importance of maintaining balance and of always knowing *who they are.* This instills within them a sense of clarity to help identify when they are exposed to negative conditions or a situation that is foreign to them. In other words, what we are trying to accomplish is giving our children a home base that they can return to if they become overwhelmed by adversity. Additionally, because you were involved in building yourself a happy life, when you sense your child is veering into dangerous territory you will have the tools to help them return home.

The weeds of life can come in various ways: they can surface from the way a teacher reprimanded your child or from the fact that your child has made a bad choice in picking a childhood friend. The important thing to get from this conversation is we must remain in our children's daily lives, proactively looking for the signs that something might be changing that needs attention.

I am blessed with three children and six grandchildren, and I have coached all of my children in several different sports for over 20 years. Additionally, as a business owner I have managed people my entire adult life and can honestly say I have enjoyed every minute of it! There have been many times within the 35 years of business ownership that I've had complete disdain for the business I chose for my career, but not once in those 35 years was my disdain directed toward my employees or the children I coached.

Since we've spent most of this chapter discussing the importance of family and the role we play as parents within our children's lives, I thought it would be appropriate to share with you a strategy I used when coaching my son and two daughters in both baseball and girl's fast pitch softball. For all you young parents getting ready to embark on the adventure of coaching, get out your pen and paper and take notes because I was not knick-named the *Phil Jackson* of kids sports for nothing! We won championships with both my son's and daughter's teams for several years in a row! What made this feat remarkable was that we did this each year with a completely different team...so I am confident the strategy works.

As mentioned, my 20-year coaching career was done at many different levels within several different sports, but I thought it best to start when my children were younger. For those of you presently coaching, I believe you will relate to my experience, especially if you are from the Midwest area of the United States. Each year the league began the process of preparing for a new season of *baseball/FP-softball* as mentioned. Because we lived in the Midwest, most of the time it was still cold in March and so tryouts were done in a local High School gym. It was a fun experience because the dads would assemble at the gym early and would start the process of razzing each other about their new method of picking that year's team, bragging how this year would produce winning results. I took a lot of incoming razing from the other dads because as I mentioned earlier, due to my success with kids we were always the team to beat.

The process of picking and preparing for the draft was a cumbersome task and was also a little nerve wracking because the system required you to know which kids were picked and which were still available. I had a good eye for talent and a system of placing kids in order that I wanted for the team, so there was never a time I was not ready when it became my turn to pick within the draft. It was a lot of fun hearing the others dads groan each time I would pick a child they wanted…usually with the response *"Damn-it, I missed that one!"*

Once we finished picking teams the dads would go over the details of who they picked, always with the expectation that this year's team was finally the team that would bring them the big prize! I recall walking out the door, satisfied I had secured a few key players that were friends of my children so they I knew they would get pleasure in telling their friends they were on the same team! My kids would always ask me if I thought we had a good team, and I would always reply with confidence that we did…knowing that once we taught the team our system we were going to be competitive.

As the new season started our first practice would generally start around mid-April, and it goes without saying that the weather in Chicago at this time was sketchy at best. I would generally start slowly with the kids, always starting with the same drills used in past seasons as this helped me assess the levels of athleticism and skill I was starting with. This was done for two reasons…the first priority was to make sure the players didn't get hurt, which would give them a bad memory early on in the season; the second goal was to convince the new team to be fearless, and so giving them drills they would have success with was critically important. As we began to build the players' self-esteem within our practices, I would begin to escalate the complexity of the drills, challenging but never discouraging the kids to take on more difficult tasks and carefully building a sense of accomplishment.

While I was assessing the level of talent of my new players, I would also begin to assess the parents, looking to spot who were going to be the problem parents for the year! For all the new coaches out there, there was a *problem parent* every new season, and after coaching a few seasons you develop a radar for spotting them within the crowd! Along with spotting the problem parents, I would also begin the process of deciphering early on the personality traits of each child on my team. Because some kids are more timid than others, this process was important in order to gradually build confidence by putting kids in positions they could handle during the early stages of their skill development.

After the first few practices, I could tell that the kids were getting comfortable with each other and our system, giving them the sense of being a team. It was at this time that I would start calling team huddles, expressing how proud I was of them and explaining that they were going to have a lot of fun during the season. Our communication within the huddles was assuring to the team. As coaches we would never yell at a team member for missing the ball, but we expected them to give their best efforts to attempt to get to the ball. The goal was to help the kids become fearless about making a mistake, and I explained that the only way they could disappoint us as coaches was to not try. To be clear…our subliminal messaging was convincing the team to understand that everyone makes mistakes, and as coaches we would never look down on them for missing the ball. However, we would be disappointed if they allowed the fear of making a mistake to keep them from trying.

During our team gatherings I would passionately look into the kids' eyes… asking them to look around the huddle at their teammates, giving them a sense of loyalty to their teammates. I explained that during the season they had to do everything they could to support our team. They had no idea what I meant at this point, so they would look at each other and smile nervously, but they were getting a sense that something special was going on. I also began to explain what I meant about never getting yelled at for trying their best, since as a team it was their obligation to try as hard as they could to make a play. If they missed the ball, they had their teammates supporting their effort. The goal was helping them to understand that it was okay to make a mistake because the team knew you gave it your best effort.

At this stage I begin to turn up the volume of motivation during our practices, attempting to get the kids comfortable diving for balls and letting them know if they missed the ball, it was a great effort! Throughout the drills we always made sure we had teammates in back-up positions, so that if they missed the ball they could count on the player behind them to make the play! This "pick up for your teammate" attitude became the theme of every practice and every play. The other coaches had no idea why the kids would yell "pick-em up" every time a teammate missed the ball, but they would soon learn this team was laser focused and was assuring their teammates that they had their backs!

Before the season began, the team's parents were beginning to buy into the program, realizing their children were having fun talking about the team and couldn't wait to get to practice or the game. Even the *problem parents* began to look at me in silence, thinking this guy might actually know what he's doing! Trust me if you can get the *problem parents* to say nothing, you have won the battle!

As we neared our first game, it was at this time that I would turn my attention to the parents, since I was confident that all the kids were in on the program. It was time to use the *energy/aura* messaging of cooperation for the parents. I made it crystal clear to the team's parents that the coaching staff would not tolerate anything but positive reinforcement for the children during the game. Additionally, in order to keep overzealous parents under control during games, I let them know we would not be looking for their input while the game was playing. The message was polite but firm: if they wanted to discuss something after the game I would be happy to meet with them, but during the game I would not allow any feelings of negativity, doubt, or second guessing to taint the kids and their positive can-do attitude and energy.

I explained to the team and their parents that we were absolutely playing to win, but what I was more concerned about was that I was sure that every player gave 100% of his or her effort while they were on the field. I let them know that if the other team beat us after we gave it our best, then we should congratulate them on their success. The big sell was convincing the kids. *As their coach* my ultimate concern was for the team to go for it on every play, and if they did we would get our share of wins!

Most seasons I felt confident my drafting selection system would produce a competitive team, but there were a few years that I had the feeling it might be a difficult season. The league was designed to cede the teams with the best record a favorable playoff schedule. Having the best record was a benefit, and we definitely tried as a team to accomplish that, but I did not let this ceding process change our strategy of building character along with creating depth in player skills from moving players around on the field. We placed a lot of importance on getting the kids exposed to and experienced in several positions on the field, and we made sure that the team understood that *win or lose,* the coaching staff would find the good things that happened during the game.

As the regular season ended and the playoffs began, our teams would arrive at the first playoff game with a look of confidence (not cockiness). They were ready and committed to fight for a *team win* because they did not fear making mistakes. As the pressure heated up and our team yelled "pick-em up" each time one of their teammates made a mistake, it became clear to the other team that nothing could discourage this team. It was an amazing transformation, year after year watching our teams once they reached the playoffs. Because of our positive messaging, these kids had developed steel in their spines! What had transpired through this process was that our teams were succeeding at accomplishing *FDR's quote of "The only thing we have to fear is fear itself"* by proving their approach to the game was fearless. Needless to say, because of their courageous fight inning after inning, never relenting or caving in to the fear of making a mistake, these kids won the prize trophy year after year.

The moral of the story is that together we can build strong families, helping one another by using this *"pick-em up"* strategy so that our children can make their way through each day with their best effort. If we focus on building strength within our children, helping them face adversity head on when it comes, they will have the same confident look in their eyes as the kids did during the playoffs.

What should be learned from this team analogy is that by preparing the team through accessing their strengths and reducing their weaknesses during the growth part of the season, I was able to create a balance of fearless and confident kids. It was a short season to prepare kids for the big game, but you as a parent have a lifetime to teach your child fearless and balanced growth using the positive moments to prepare them for the big game!

CHAPTER 11

Emotional IQ

The world of psychology has dissected the human species and our characteristic traits into a plethora of categories. Our emotions or response mechanisms to a situation are said to determine how we handle that situation based on the character traits we possess. Many of us think of characteristic traits as *jealousy, envy, vindictiveness, shyness, gregariousness, resentment assertiveness, etc.*. In terms of Psychology CIA Character-In-Action created a chart separating human character traits by dividing them into 66 different emotional characteristics. As you can see by the chart, the ones we have defined as traits are not on this chart.

The traits I listed in the first paragraph are what I define as personality traits and it is my belief that personality traits decide how we will grow as a person and in large part decide which of the 66 characteristic traits displayed above will become part of our lives. As an observant parent understanding this list of defining personality traits, you may be surprised by how early personality traits begin developing within your child's life. By studying their interaction with you as the parent, with their siblings, and in an open social setting with a group of children, you can visually see the genetic traits they carry and how they will ultimately use these traits to handle problem solving, achievements, and interactions throughout their life.

Many people view their children in play groups and other settings, letting their child act freely with the thought that this is part of their development and will help them to hone their interactive skills. If a parent sees their child grabbing a toy from another child, they nicely say "we share," and eventually he or she will learn that they are expected to share with others.

If we look closely as our children interact with others, we will start to see defining moments in which the weeds we discussed earlier start taking shape. It is my belief that harvesting the best crop starts as early as in these childhood social settings. By studying your child's interaction early on, this will give you insight as a parent about which personality traits you need to strengthen and which ones should be toned down. The goal as a parent should be to provide your child with balance, because balance allows children to experience and use as many of the 66 characteristic traits to achieve success and friendship throughout their lives.

I use the saying "for every action there is a reaction" in almost every thought and action I do throughout my life. I do not use it in terms of manipulation but as a source to find peaceful outcomes either before or after I am involved in a given situation. In other words, if I am faced with a problem that needs a solution, before I finalize what I consider the solution I try to consider the reaction I will get to the action I take attempting to solve the problem. The key to problem solving is making sure your solution to the problem does not bring you more problems. In parallel, if I am creating a policy I try to understand the impact it will have on the various people involved and how they will be affected by it. It is my contention that if as a general rule we understand and consider both the personality and characteristic traits of the people we are dealing with when making a decision, we can have a better outcome to the "action/reaction" process.

As we continue, I am going to ask you to get in touch with the personality traits you have and to define which trait dominates the power of your decisions/motives. My goal is to make your life less complicated by helping you create your own "action/reaction" regarding how you solve problems or interact with people. If we can identify our dominant traits that prejudge our first response mechanism determining how we approach thinking or solving a problems, we will have more balance within the solutions/outcomes we create.

Let's reflect back to the chapter "Do you control your mind or does your mind control you?," in which we stressed that everything we discuss regarding *personality/characteristic* traits again falls to the power of thought or recognition of our thought. The problem with most of us is that we believe we cannot change outcomes because we are predestined to continue on a path that has been consistent throughout our lives. In other words, we allow our thoughts or habits of the past to send a subliminal message to how we react to a situation, thereby setting ourselves up for a poor result in the *action/reaction* response.

Psychologists/psychiatrists have lucrative careers because the complexity of what happens within a patient's mind is usually beyond their understanding. In my view, what has developed over time within the world of psychology is that rather than identify and seek a real solution to a patient's struggle, therapists have developed a system of counseling or managing their patient's lives on a visit-to-visit basis. Additionally, rather than making clear to the patient which trait (or motive of trait) is responsible for creating their ongoing problems, many doctors are using prescription drugs to numb or lower the anxiety of using or relying on a dominant negative trait.

If we analyze the severity of mental health problems in America, referring back to subliminal advertising messaging, we should view this process through the *action/reaction* result as to its impact on our children. Reviewing the average life of an American family, we see that often both parents must work in order to pay their bills. The result is that many children are dropped off daily at day-care centers all across the country. Some may be more fortunate in that they have a grandparent or aunt to watch them during the day, but a large percentage are raised with other children and adults whom they relate to only peripherally. Let's consider the *action/reaction* response when parents are not able to help shape the lives of their children during these critical early years. When parents miss their child's interaction time with other children they lose their chance to see their child's developing personality traits early on. In addition, no help is forthcoming from the employees of the *day care center,* who do not have a clue about the blueprint of your child's responses. Therefore there is little thought put forth to understand an individual child's dominant personality trait(s) and how to best mold them for the child's future.

Although the *day care* center employee is probably skilled at keeping your child safe and being sure he or she has things to do, he or she does not know the inner workings of your child's blueprint. You are the only one best qualified to identify specific personality traits in your child that might match your own or traits from your spouse, parents, siblings, or even your in-laws. You as the parent have unique experiences within your family circle that can help you identify and relate to how your child might react to something, giving you the unique ability to help create balance to your child's *reaction to an action.*

Please do not misconstrue the message…I understand that many families have no choice but to have both parents work. My hope is if we discuss these things and understand their significance it will help prompt us to use the time we have with our children more wisely. If we are aware of the different traits and have the ability to see when certain traits start to dominate how our child responds to their action/reaction interaction, it will help us pull out the weeds, thus giving your child balance.

Children are a gift to humanity and helping them grow in order to achieve their full potential of friendship, relationships with their spouse, and advancement within their career is a gift every parent or guardian should cherish. Having said that, it is now time to discuss our own traits and how we as adults function within our social circles. We must also learn how we identify and pull weeds that have grown within our lives as a result of the barrage of subliminal messaging.

When it comes to adults I like to discuss personality traits in the form of the aura surrounding us while we interact with people or while we're doing an activity we may like or dislike. To better explain what I mean by an aura...think of a glowing light surrounding you as glowing brightly when you are functioning well and dimming when you seem to be struggling. As we get further along with this *aura* I am describing we will be using it as a visual, helping you to see and feel as you begin to understand how it works in relation to interacting with other people.

This *aura* I speak of can and should also be thought of as a *positive and negative flow of energy* that transforms between people as they interact. The best scenario or description for this *energy/aura* that reacts between two people in a positive sense is when the energy flows between two people it should flow equally. When this happens, even though it is between two separate people, we should visualize the energy connecting as one. In other words, the strength of this energy increases significantly when it meets an equal energy source, allowing it to reach its full potential.

Conversely, when we meet someone that we don't like or communicate with well, we would see the glow of this *energy/aura* being reduced drastically. As we move along with our discussion on how this *energy/ aura* works, we will talk about how to identify personality traits you carry and how we either help or hinder a good energy flow with our friends and family members.

As we start this process, I will ask with the question: *"Are you a giver or taker of energy?"* Remember how we've discussed the importance of seeing *energy* as a visual thing; this will help us begin to identify whether the people surrounding you are givers or takers of your energy!

At this time I would like you to go through each of your family and friends one at a time and visualize your last civil conversation with them. What I mean by civil is a conversation where you may have found agreement, a beneficial conversation exchanging thoughts. I would like you to do this visualization with all your family members and in time five of your closest friends. Once we get the process done, you can start analyzing the energy flow between the people you work with and others.

We will start with your parents, since they are always the easiest to pick on! The balance of energy between a parent and a child is something many parents never quite grasp because many times parents speak at their children rather than speak with them, but for an example of *energy stealers* they are good to start with.

If we break this down even further you may find that you bring certain subjects to Mom for discussion and others to Dad, based on who will provide you with the best insight regarding a subject. This may happen because our parents may have a closed mind to the topic you would like to discuss, and so you go to the best suited parent for this discussion. What happens during this process of parent picking is that you are knowingly seeking to engage in a conversation of exchange that allows you to easily express your thoughts and feelings while gaining the wisdom of someone else's thoughts regarding the topic.

Younger readers could probably relate to this by thinking of who to talk to about the latest update on a computer program. We live in a world of technology where interactive apps are made by different technology companies to coincide with the original hard drive. In order for this to happen our computers must be frequently updated because the dialogue between the hard drive and the new app must learn how to function together without interruptions getting back to picking *Mom or Dad* regarding a topic you wish to discuss. I am assuming at this point that everyone reading this book is an adult, so I won't insult you by saying that you've gone to one parent more than the other because you will get what you want as an outcome. This energy I speak of is for the purpose of equal exchange between two adults seeking to have a beneficial conversation to help one another.

Getting back to why you may have picked one parent over another is you have knowingly already visualized through your selection process that if you spoke to Dad about getting an apartment with your newly acquired boyfriend, he would most likely have entered the conversation by sucking all the air out of the room. In other words, Dad would consume your aura/energy, leaving you with a feeling of emptiness regarding the subject of getting an apartment, while your inner self says Mom would be easier or more accepting to the having a conversation.

This example is extreme, but helps visualization and understanding the concept of exchange between two people. To get further into the description of family and friends, we will move to a conversation with a sibling. Often older siblings become what I refer to as energy stealers because they have the power of having been born first so that their connection with Mom and Dad is better than yours. They also have had the advantage of knowing the rules before you did, and this gives them the ability to join Mom and Dad in telling you what to do. Last, the advantage they have over you is something they like and in many cases they will do all they can, even as adults to hold on to: the premise that *"I was born first, I am older than you";* therefore I have power over you.

In most cases people go along never addressing this issue or asking the older sibling for advice, preferring to let them know that you are both adults and the power they had as a child no longer exists. It is important to address this and get past that hurdle because there is no better ally than a family member as a friend for life. Many people sign off on their brother or sister because they don't appreciate their condescending attitude, although most times it's nothing more than a conversation setting the timetable to adulthood rather than a sibling rivalry. Once you carefully get your older sibling to know you love them and to respect you for your *"Gift"* and you respect them for theirs…there is no greater bond of friendship!

How do we choose a best friend? A best friend is thought of as someone we have things in common with but if you use our method of discovering the aura between you and your *"best friend"* it is generally a person you find comfort and mutual agreement with during your conversations. Many of you will tell your best friend just about anything… knowing they will not judge you, and if they do, they know how to best deliver their judgment in a kind way.

Again, I would like to visualize what is happening with the energy flow between you and your friend. If we were to think of the depiction of angels in literature, they are generally shown with a spiritual aura around them signifying that they are heavenly. If we envision that same *angel aura* around you and your friend, we can take it one step further by visualizing the two auras connecting and transferring equally back and forth, never leaving one and staying with the other… This explains why you chose this person to be your best friend. It is two people accepting one another as they are with a mutual thought of helping each other to be stronger without a beneficial gain for oneself.

Now it is time to discuss the people we know within our daily lives. People who for some reason each time we converse with them we feel utterly depleted and get no sense of satisfaction from the conversation. I call these people the *"energy stealers,"* and if we define them through their personality traits, many times they are folks who are envious, jealous, dominant, and insecure. What they do either knowingly or unknowingly is actually attempt to steal your aura because of their need for other people to be weak so that they can feel strong. It is important to understand that the people riddled with these overpowering personality traits cannot find strength unless others around them are weak. The people that end up as friends to the *"energy stealers"* are those who are timid by nature or have low self-esteem, believing that somehow their opinion is not as valuable as others.

The folks looking to steal energy are generally the kids we spoke of earlier who have not had a parent or guardian available to curb their unproductive personality traits, thus creating an improper balance. Changing them can be difficult for parents because in many cases these kids are strong willed; therefore it requires extra effort to tame the personality traits that can bring the children negativity throughout their adult lives. People carrying these personality traits often struggle to have successful marriages or find it difficult to get promoted in business to obtain higher positions that require teamwork. If the *"energy stealers"* are successful in business, it is generally hard for them to hold on to long-term employees because of their tendency to attack others.

On the opposite side of the *"energy stealers"* we have the *"energy givers"*; these folks are generally timid by nature and cannot create much energy/aura because of their low self-esteem. These people are always apologizing and feeling each time they speak they must clarify what they meant to be sure they do not offend you. They are generally nice people but one is never really sure how they feel about something, so not many people seek out the *giver* to be a best friend or have a long-term relationship with. The relationship is a match of two people connecting with one who consumes all of the other's energy, leaving the *giver* completely depleted.

If we return to our conversation regarding our responsibility as a parent, remember that you are the architect of your child's blueprint. Because you know *who you are* and what you feel and also have a pretty good understanding of your spouse, you are uniquely qualified to identify characteristic traits within your child from both sides of the family. It is critical to catch harmful traits early on, doing all we can to create balance for our children by offsetting the power of a dominant trait.

It is a delicate balance and requires and understanding of your child early on. I like to think of this in terms of opposites, so if we think of a simple personality trait such as *"selfish,"* we think of the opposite trait as being *"giving."* Or by using the term *"shy"* we can then use the opposite term *"gregarious."* If we as parents can identify the dominant traits of our child early on, this will allow us to coax them along, attempting to get them comfortable with a little bit of the opposite trait. Remember that the key things we are attempting to do is find our child's *gift* and to identify his or her dominant traits. The goal is to help your children identify the things that seem to come easy to them and to give them balance within their social life in order to reduce anxiety as much as possible.

Remembering what we learned in the chapter *"Do you control your brain, or does your brain control you?"* we know that the things we do as a person are not predestined. For those of you who are stuck in life and using the excuse, *"I have the worst luck…things just don't work out easy for me,"* my belief is there is no such thing as good luck or bad luck. Life is determined by good decisions or bad decisions. If you are a person who believes your life is what it is because of poor luck, it is time to own the thoughts and decisions you made to get you where you are today.

The reason I named this chapter "Emotional IQ" is because I believe emotions should be controlled by the power of thought, and once we learn to master the control of our thoughts we can master the control of our emotions. I am not suggesting that we live a life of preplanned boredom without any spontaneous emotional responses. What I am suggesting is that we analyze our own lives in the same way we analyzed our children's, pulling the weeds in our own personal lives. When I discuss Emotional IQ it is a discussion of us being aware of *who we are* and using our *gift* to help us achieve a *balance* within our character traits without ever allowing one trait to dominate the always creating the same outcome. This requires us to analyze and be truthful with ourselves regarding the thoughts we have. If we know what our traits are and we take a moment to think how we will control the *action/reaction* of our response, we will achieve better outcomes to life situations. Last, if we understand the *aura/energy* we give or take and how it is affecting others we can collectively work at sharing our *aura/energy* and trying to create a harmonious glow with those close to us, helping to build long-lasting relationships. By working at improving and understanding our energy field we will also be able to better recognize and identify the *energy stealers* who are seeking to sabotage your *aura*, leaving you with a feeling of insignificance.

All of these things we discussed do not require counselling or drugs prescribed by a doctor, they merely require you to self-analyze, realizing and practicing the things that you know come easy to you, and recognizing and learning to control your dominant traits in the attempt to find balance. By understanding the concept of equal exchange we do not have to accept our lives with a predetermined outcome. What I am suggesting is not a difficult task: if you can control your mind to turn a light switch on and off then you can control your mind to turn off a harmful emotion or anxious moment, and the first step to doing this is to understand the aura/energy concept!

CHAPTER 12

BEAUTY IS INTERNAL

W hen a child is born, the parents who have anxiously awaited the birth of their newborn fall in love the minute he or she arrives. For just an instant this newborn child upon entering the new world receives only love, completely free from prejudice. The parents of the newborn are solely interested in the health of the child and the well-being of the mother after experiencing the traumatic experience of childbirth.

If they are fortunate enough to have the doctor give both the baby and the mother a thumbs up, the next stage of parenting begins. Both parents begin to look at the baby with amazement and think how incredible it is that two people can be joined as one to create another human bearing each of their DNA. They also begin to look at their baby closely, laughing and full of love and trying to determine who this baby looks like!

Mom looks closely the newborn and says to Dad "I think *he or she* has your nose"! Dad is proud and full of joy the baby might have one of his physical traits and may toss back a compliment to Mom saying the baby has her dimples, or maybe her eyes. However, what is really happening within the first few days of the newborn's life is a judgment of *his or her* looks. As time goes on, the features of the child begin to form more clearly, defining to society a person with a unique and individual outer shell. Additionally, what has transpired is the parents of this newborn no longer see the child through *his or her* looks but through the beauty of the child's soul. The parents have now grown to love the child from the inside, and although they may see cosmetic traits resembling themselves they understand that their child is uniquely their own.

What a beautiful life it would be if only the world could view us through our parent's eyes. If you ask most parents who among their children is the prettiest or the most handsome, they would look at you astonished, thinking how could you ask such a dumb question. In other words, what has happened for the parents is that the *beauty of all their children has become internalized.* Parents love their children unconditionally not based on looks or brains but on the love for the child for who they are as a person.

What we learn from history is as the human species continued to progress we understand how we look, began to play a significant role within individual human advancement. Research shows that women's cosmetics date back 6000 years! This is an amazing thought when you think how hard it must have been just to survive 6000 years ago. Of course, it was only for a few of the ruling class women who had the time and resources to use products for beauty. None the less, this is when the process of enhancing one's features began.

Hollywood has generated films depicting ancient human existence showing how there were class systems from the beginning of civilization. On Easter Sunday throughout America, many homes turn on their televisions to watch Hollywood's historic documentation of *The Ten Commandments.* Most of us understand the religious significance of the film, but what should also be understood is the display of a social class system and of Nefertiti's beauty shown for all the people to see.

As the soldiers carried Nefertiti through the crowds, many women would look upon her and see her beauty and her privilege and wonder what it must be like to live a life of royalty. Some would attempt to use the resources they had available to cosmetically enhance their beauty in an attempt to emulate Nefertiti..

The men carrying swords who received favor from and protected the Pharaoh at this time were men of great physical attributes. . Men within the working class looked upon these soldiers and understood that they achieved their position of stature as a result of their physical attributes and abilities.

What we learn from this is that no matter what period of time we examine within recorded history, there has been from the beginning of time subliminal messaging influencing people to change *who they are and how they look* based on clues they receive from a ruling class. Additionally, the common denominator of the ruling class throughout history has been the power and control of currency and the ability to create and enforce law among its citizens, thus controlling the messages and laws delivered to the masses. Often the power and force of the military were used to enforce their messaging..

Throughout my writing I've continued to make the case that we as citizens are being *set up to fail.* I would much prefer a discussion of the positive things transpiring within our country but because of the power and control of an ever-present dangerous messaging system that is influencing large segments of the population, I feel compelled to warn my fellow citizens of its threat.. Many of you reading this book inherently know that America's freedom and independence will not sustain itself if we continue to accept dysfunction and disarray as a normal state of being.

The question we must answer as a people is what should be considered normal and what should be defined as dysfunctional? I approach this subject with extreme caution because we are seeing through identity politics that our nation is being divided into categories in order to establish what our politicians refer to as their voting base. The division of our nation's people has become extremely dangerous because the subliminal messaging we receive is not a message of what brings us together...but a clear message of what divides us.

My belief is whatever category you fall into as defined by our politicians, we as a people must come together to decide how we will allow our country to be governed in the future. If we allow the politicians to continue to pit one group against the other then we must accept our government's goal of reducing our power to effect change. By allowing them to divide us, we are relinquishing our strength as a unified citizenship and giving our government the ability to become an all-powerful central government.

I have carefully laid out the infrastructure of the principles America was originally built on, along with exposing those seeking to reduce your *energy/aura* through dominance. I have also emphasized the importance of understanding and controlling your personality traits so that they do not hinder your state of mental health. We have discussed pulling the weeds of dysfunction in our lives in order to reap the best harvest we can from our *individual gifts*. Whether you are white, black, rich, poor, gay, straight, or any other identity, we must agree that using these principles can help guide us to a life of stability.

Without being judgmental my hope is to open the minds of those who may feel suppressed by others. There are many other people who feel as you do, and we have outlined the things you can do to feel better about your mental state and your country.. We must not allow television programs to guide us into believing that lawlessness, the worship of money, our separation into defined opposing groups, or using Hollywood as the definition of a normal society is okay.

If we consider Hollywood as an elite society, we can compare it to the example used regarding the messaging sent from Pharaoh to his people. The greatest political and social pressures appear to be on women. Like ancient cultures who revered women of beauty, mothers and daughters in America receive a similar message through television. The idea that beauty is measured by what women look like from the outside and not what is within their hearts and souls is a loud and clear message delivered by Hollywood and the world of fashion.

The vision of half-starved young girls and young men displaying the latest fashions on runways all over the world, bringing the latest fashions to the elites, is disturbing. Behind these displays of external beauty is the same thing that drives all advertisements... *the sale of products at the expense of human worth.*

It seems innocent enough to see these young women strutting the runway displaying beautiful smiles walking on 4-inch heals to provide a better visual effect for the new fashions. This messaging seems harmless enough, but as we dissect the *action/reaction* we begin to understand how damaging this "show" is to these models.

The images of these young women go beyond the runways...they hit fashion magazines sold everywhere, touching many aspects of our lives. The enticements of these beautiful models also may cause expectations of what men feel women should look like. Additionally, the constant exposure women receive from this barrage of advertisements begins to create expectations within themselves on how they should look; this ultimately damages their self-esteem when they cannot achieve the results of the images displayed.

What most of us forget is how little these fixed-up photos actually represent the person in real life. Most of us only get the chance to see these highly paid stars and models within their made-up world, representing their life of fantasy to the masses of innocent people as if it is their reality.

Throughout our discussion I will continue to provide examples demonstrating the reality of our existence that *are in fact setting you up to fail!* The messaging we receive from all these sources is there is always something better than what we already possess. If we understand the goal of successful advertising, it is designed to entice you into feeling that something is missing in your life.. This creates anxiety and the feeling that action must be taken in order to provide satisfaction to your need for whatever product they are selling. These *advertisers* are working overtime attempting to discover selling methods that will make you desire their product, leading to anxiety and frustration..

I will feel accomplished if I've done nothing more than to convince you to open your eyes to the *rat race* underlying the daily onslaught of subliminal messaging. We must understand that the anxiety we feel is not because we are freaks riddled with psychological disorders. A good deal of it is from the barrage of advertising we are exposed to daily, always with the attempt to stir a sensation of need or want to buy something we don't have. Life should be more than what we own or possess; it should be the creation of positive life experiences through positive *energy/aura* traded equally with people we love. Beauty should not be judged by what we appear on the outside but what we deliver from the inside. If we try to view others through the eyes of a parent, seeking to find the beauty inside everyone we meet…our world would be a far better place!

As we have also discussed throughout this book… is that it is extremely difficult to deal with the daily onslaught of negative news. In addition to the reports of terrorism around the world, Americans receive daily reports from politicians stating that our debt as a country is unsustainable and that our financial institutions are subject to collapse if changes don't happen soon. American families are also now tormented by the idea that someone could steal their child or he or she could be abused by an adult, plus we are saddened and frightened by the number of school killings of children that have occurred in recent years.

I could go on and on, listing the daily assaults delivered by our media/politicians to the American citizens. I could continue by describing the barrage of unhealthy food commercials, or the frequency of the prescription drugs industry promoting their latest drug, or even the legal firm notifying you that the drugs you were prescribed are dangerous to your health. My message within this chapter is if you have done all you can to survive this storm of advertising, you've managed to keep your weight at a healthy level, and you haven't completely lost your mind, then that is a huge success!

As we go on…let's not be distressed by the false advertisements from Hollywood and the fashion industry attempting to promote a look of perfection. Let's be smart enough to realize that before photo-editing or other enhancements used to give us the image of perfection that the people we see on the movie screen or on magazine covers are not very different from you. We have nothing to be ashamed of, and the truth is our *beauty* is judged by our friends, families, and coworkers not by how we look but by the things we do and say as people.

CHAPTER 13

Determine the Size
of Your Tank

L et's discuss applying *thought* control to handle being overweight. There's no debate that some of us are more genetically prone to weight gain than others, but using *thought* control can help us better choose the foods we eat, along with controlling our portion size. We have discussed balancing our lives in order to achieve mental health, and learning how to control our weight is one more aspect of our lives that I believe is worth a discussion.

Based on diet and lifestyle, many American's now have a propensity to weight gain or obesity. Based on the statistics we read a large percentage of Americans are now struggling with obesity. There are several different reasons being debated as to why: the experimentation of our foods by modern science, the provision of poor quality food high in trans-fat by the fast food industry, a sedentary lifestyle, and finally our overindulgence at every meal...eating as though it is our last meal!

There are a number of books written regarding the unhealthy diet the American people eat, but before we deal with what we are eating we must learn *to control* our impulses to overeat brought on by subliminal messaging from the *food industry advertisers*. In the last paragraph, I listed several legitimate reasons contributing to America's obesity, but regardless of the food we choose, the amount we consume is the number one culprit to weight gain. The good news is that overconsumption is something we can solve by using *thought* control!

When I was a child the rules my parents used regarding meals was, *"Do not to leave the table until you have finish everything on your plate!"* Growing up in the 1960's usually the father worked while the mother took care of the home along with preparing meals for the family. Depending on the time of year (i.e., being in school or on summer break), almost every day my brother and I found a way to practice or play whatever sport we were engaged in at the time just before dinner began. Once we were called in for dinner, the portion size of each serving was dictated by our parents to assure we would maintain our energy and good health.

Each family had their own method regarding who was the *"eat your food enforcer"* during dinner in our home...Dad was the *"enforcer,"* and Mom was in charge of governing how we filled our plate, always stating *"you need to eat more...you're a growing boy."* Depending on the food being served, this was either a good thing or in my case 50% of the time it was a bad thing! The general summation from parents back then was that a big appetite was a sign of good health; therefore most parents urged their children to eat more. Since there was little *fast or fake food* (GMOs) during this time and people were more active, the impact from overeating was not as significant it is today. As we discussed earlier, today's action/reaction of less exercise along with the change from *real food* to fast (fake) or genetically modified food is something each of us should be aware of when making food choices.

We're going to use another visual in order to incorporate *"do you control your mind or does your mind control you?"* regarding weight control. Most of you either own or are aware of what an automobile is…I thought we could use a car as our visual prop to discuss individual weight control. The average car in America generally has a 15- to 20-gallon gas tank. The miles per gallon vary per car based on the engine size and how each individual driver accelerates the gas pedal. It is common knowledge that if we drive slowly and steadily the car will consume far less gas than if we put the peddle to the metal, thus flooding a large amount of gas into the cylinder heads and pushing the engine to its limits.

You probably have already begun to understand where I am going with this visual! Using *thought* control, we're going to use the automobile as a crude example to help us to understand the impact of how much we eat plus the amount of activity we do daily to communicate the importance of burning your body's fuel before refilling the tank. First, let's imagine going to the gas station to fill up our car's gas tank; we are putting 20gallons of gas into our automobile's 15-gallon tank. The result would be gas overflowing from the tank over the entire gas station parking lot.

We can use the same visualization for putting too much food into our bodies, filling our stomach beyond the size of its tank. Like what occurred in the gas station parking lot, the extra food would overflow within our body's parking lot…only it is stored as excess fat! Having said that, I do believe the process of understanding the consequences of the *action/reaction* regarding weight control should start with discipline *(appetite control)*. We should understand that the food we eat (similar to our automobile's needing gas) is nothing more than fuel needed to keep our bodily functions working effectively.

We are subjected daily to a barrage of advertising displaying new diets or showing us the latest exercise craze that will help us shed the extra pounds. Some of these diets advertise… *"you can eat all you want and still lose weight!"* Medical institutions have joined in the battle of weight control by offering bariatric surgery, an operation that actually reduces the size of your stomach! What this medical procedure means is that by reducing the size of our stomachs *(tank size)* and thus eliminating overindulging, we will avoid overflowing and lose weight.

A large percentage of healthy infants are born with a stomach that is specifically sized to fit his or her newborn body. It is not until the infant starts to become an adolescent and then becomes an adult that his or her stomach size begins to change based on eating habits. That is why I believe it is important for each of us to recognize/visualize how big a normal size stomach should be. By understanding this we can start to analyze the amount of food we consume, visualizing how the meal size we eat will fit within our stomachs without increasing its size.

To explain this process a little better, what happens as we prepare to eat is our brain sends messages to our stomach (which is considered a muscle) to relax the muscle, allowing the stomach to increase its size if necessary. There are medical reports stating the stomach can be stretched five times its normal size. So, if we use the visualization of our stomach starting at the size of a quart of milk, we can further visualize it expanding to the size of a gallon of milk! After the meal is completed, the digestive process begins and the stomach will begin to recede... but now the process of stressing the digestive organs begins.

I understand the premise of *thought control* sounds too simple, and for some of us the taste of food is far too stimulating and enjoyable to limit portion sizes. Your view may be that you will suffer the consequences and do a little extra exercise to burn off the extra calories. The problem is that the extra food you ate will not be dealt with until your body recognizes a drastic decrease in consumption, along with a drastic increase in burning calories beyond the food you are consuming. What is critically important to understand is that this external battle you face by eating too much one day and then attempting to eat less another day becomes a major stressor to our bodies' internal organs.

At this point our brain may become dangerous and actually does begin to prepare to make unhealthy decisions in advance. This is also why identifying our impulses and learning to control our *thoughts* is critical. If we react to and allow the overeating impulse because we like how something might taste, our brain takes over handling the action/reaction to the act of overeating. Next our internal organs are directed to function as our brain begins to calculate the process of digestion and our brain signals to the digestive organs what they must do to clean up after the trauma of overeating. Your internal organs do the best they can to handle the over-abundance of food but your brain realizes there is more food than your system can handle, so the process of storing fat begins.

If we return to the visual of putting 20gallons of gas in our automobile's 15-gallon tank, I believe it's safe to assume none of us would ever do such a thing, and we certainly wouldn't do it over and over. It is critical for each of you to determine your tank (stomach) size and then calculate how much food it requires to fill the tank. If you see that you are carrying external fat, this is your body's signal to you that you have been overfilling your tank.

In order to determine our tank/stomach size. Let's start with another visual. The average size stomach is approximately 12" long and 6" wide at the widest part. It should hold approximately 1 quart if you were to fill it with purely liquid. Please take a moment to visualize turning a quart of milk on its side across your upper abdomen region and then, taking it a step further, considering the portion size of food it would take to fill this quart container. Once we realize the size of a normal stomach, we can begin to make better judgments about portion sizes we eat to properly fit into this holding tank (stomach) without causing it to stretch!

If we understand the concept of overeating, the result of filling our stomach beyond its normal size…is that we have essentially predetermined but ignored the overflow entering into our bodies. For those struggling with the thought of eating smaller portions, my suggestion is to start by decreasing the meal sizes and slightly increasing the frequency of your meals. By doing this, you will allow your digestive system to complete its job at the first meal, thus reducing stress to your internal organs that are attempting to digest food beyond their capabilities.

The second part of our discussion is the sedentary lifestyle of many Americans. If we view the food we eat as nothing more than fuel in numerical calories, applying the math to how many calories we consume daily and then maintain a cardiovascular exercise for 30 to45 minutes daily, we should be able to analyze how many calories we consume and how many calories we burn. There is no other way to accomplish maintaining a steady balanced weight, eliminating the ups and downs except by making a commitment to stop overfilling our tank, making sure we have actively used the calories already eaten before consuming more.

To those of you who love food…the discussion we are having is not an attempt to discourage you from enjoying all the delightful dishes available. My point is simple…eating should be considered fuel needed for your body to properly function. If we eat too little you may suffer malnutrition and fatigue, and if we eat too much we can *damage or stress* internal organs from the constant demand of working overtime. Our diet is no different than anything else we discussed thus far and should be thought of it in terms of balance. Our action of eating should trigger the action of being sure we have properly used the fuel we've consumed. This should be structured into the way we live our lives. Many critics may attempt to dispel my theory of *thought* control to win the fight against obesity. We must remember that obesity is a cash cow (no pun intended) to the *"advertisers of food."* If we consider the profits generated from obesity…we begin to see why once more subliminal messaging is attacking our human impulses. It's a *win/win* for the *"diet and fast food industry"* because both diet and fast food win once they get you to act upon your impulses. The greatest danger to the "advertisers of evil" is a citizenship with the ability to understand and control their impulses of binge eating and overindulging.

My goal is to help you achieve a positive mental state of mind. Many Americans are struggling daily because *they are being set up to fail.* If each of us can use the visuals we discussed by understanding the size of our tank (stomach) and determine how many miles per gallon burn (activity burning up calories), we can effectively manage how much we should eat. We must remember for *every action there is a reaction*…if you decide to overfill your tank, the result is always the same…the overage floods into the bodies' parking lot and stays that way until we actively clean it up by consuming less and increasing our activity to burn more calories.

Achieving a healthy weight and good mental health requires a lifetime of proper eating habits and a consistent program of regular exercise. Please don't let anyone attempt to fool you into believing there is an easier way. Every person's body burns the fuel they consume at a different pace…the important thing to discover is how you can create balance in your individual diet. Don't fool yourself by thinking once you are successful at reducing your weight that it will stay that way without maintaining a balance of consumption and reduction through exercise. Remember your weight is no different than your thoughts…you must decide ***are you in control of your weight or is your weight in control of you!***

CHAPTER 14

ACCEPTANCE

When I think back and reflect upon the one significant lesson I learned that helped me to change my life and brought me happiness in my daily existence, the answer is simple…I learned to laugh at myself! What a relief it was once I learned how to get off my own back and realized that no one is perfect and some of the things we believe to be so important are actually funny!

What comes along with the personality trait of being an introverted person is that over time they may become extremely rigid in social settings because the last thing they want to do is draw attention to themselves. If attention becomes centered around the *introverted/shy* person, they often become uncomfortable or overprotective of their actions; their extreme seriousness causes them to lock up even more until the situation passes. They also tend to become more protective or guarded in the future in order to ensure they are not subjected to that kind of embarrassment again.

So I cannot stress enough the importance of learning how to laugh at yourself. I believe this to be so significant that I will stress again and again that a person cannot find happiness in life without having the ability to laugh at him or herself.

Let's recall the story I shared earlier regarding my method of coaching kids. If you remember my main focus in the beginning was to convince the children to do nothing more than take the risk of trying their best to make a play. I didn't pressure them to make the play…I just wanted them to risk without inhibition going beyond what they perceived they could do. What I didn't mention was that I knew most of the kids wouldn't take the risk because they were afraid of missing the ball and being judged by their *teammates/peers* for not making the play.

We've dedicated time thus far learning *"who we are"* and discussing how to acknowledge or discover our *gift*. If we can discover our *gifts*, realizing what it is what comes easy to each of us, we can then learn to accept and excel within the perimeters of these *gifts*. The important thing to understand is that it's okay if you are not the best at everything. It is also okay if the friends or coworkers you surround yourself with perform better than you do at the things you find difficult. If we create relationships with people around us we care about and openly share our *aura/power*, they will help us to achieve better results with our shortfalls. What's even more crucial is having the ability to laugh at our shortfalls, knowing that each of us have unique good qualities.

God grant me the serenity to accept the things I cannot change; courage to change the things I can; and wisdom to know the difference.

I've titled this chapter "Acceptance" because the word itself has great meaning and can be used in a multitude of ways. You can read every chapter in this book considering whether you will accept the value of my thoughts. You can look also upon yourself and recognize your strengths and weaknesses and decide whether you accept them for what they are. You can look upon every important decision you've made in your lifetime, good and bad, and either accept or reject the result of the action/reaction to the decision.

We should realize that acceptance is a not weakness but a strength. By accepting whatever it is that has transpired within your life (good or bad), you will have the ability to analyze these events and move on. We need look no further than the life of an addict. The first stage for any person suffering from some form of addiction is to accept the fact that they are an addict. If we reflect upon the thought of addiction, it is easy for us to understand that the premise of accepting and admitting to addiction must happen before we can heal from the affliction.

Life can be extremely difficult, and we may be exposed to numerous unforeseen stumbling blocks. If we analyze how we got past our problems, we begin to realize that this process must always start by accepting whatever it is that initiated the dilemma. If we look upon something and continuously deny or ignore it exists, then we cannot honestly hope for it to change.

Let's reflect back to the discussion of weight control. There's no question that some people are more genetically prone to weight gain, but if those people *accept* their genetic heritage, this acceptance will help them make better decisions regarding their *action/reaction* to overeating. If you *accept* the fact that you may be genetically prone to weight gain, you must also *accept* that it was your choice to consume more food than your body could metabolize, which will cause a *reaction to the action* of overeating. This is not a statement of insensitivity...there are some people who have medical reasons as to why their bodies do not properly metabolize food. Yet even for these folks it becomes more important to understand and *accept* their bodies' performance and to realize that weight loss for them is a lifestyle change they must take on for life if they hope to maintain a steady weight.

Continuing on the discussion of acceptance, if we reflect on the serenity prayer and break down its meaning, it starts with *"God give me the serenity to accept the things I cannot change."* It is important to understand the meaning of this phrase: it is to accept *change* after you have exhausted all your efforts of helping to make sure the change works effectively. There will be times we may not agree with the result and impact of a change, but once it is set and no longer up for debate… we must accept it.

The latter part of the serenity prayer was the *"courage to change the things I can; and wisdom to know the difference."* Having "wisdom" is the key word within the *action/ reaction* process of the serenity prayer. Wisdom is what determines how we react to change…it tells us in our heart when it is time to keep on fighting or to accept change. If we continue to fight something after there is no chance of creating a different outcome, it is at this point that the lack of acceptance becomes a detriment. Many people become bitter and resentful because they cannot accept the change, which is not a good outcome.

Once we reach this state, making decisions based on resentment, we are allowing our minds to be controlled by our impulses. If we apply wisdom as the serenity prayer suggests by accepting the things we cannot change and moving on to the things we can, our lives becomes much less frustrating and much more effective.

There is no greater challenge to accept than when we lose someone we love. This is by far the greatest burden placed upon us. This points to why living a life of bitterness and resentment has no value. Many of us go on each day without a consideration of the value of the lives of loved ones surrounding us, and it is not until they are gone that we begin to reflect upon and appreciate the value they brought to our lives.

People around the world face the challenge of losing someone they love every single day. Losing a loved one is one of the few consistent events that cause us to reflect on how we may have treated someone or whether or not we let them know while they were here how much they meant to us. It is the acceptance of understanding that we will all one day die that should shake the ground we walk on, causing us to reflect on the value of how we live. If we accept the terms that all are all mortal should we not also accept the terms that we will strive for a life of value and acceptance.

The differences we have with others or the resentment filling our lives all but disappears when it comes time to meeting our maker. The thought that there are no more tomorrows seems to be the only thing that can change a hardened heart. My call to all humanity is that we must not wait until death in order to appreciate life. Should the love of oneself or the love of money come before those we love? My notion is not to stop striving for oneself or to be driven by success but to place the ones we love as the main reason we strive to succeed, letting them know how much we love them and thereby teaching them that the value of life comes before the value of all else.

If our foundation and appreciation for life are based on the understanding of our mortality, it becomes more important to measure our lives not by our individual achievements but by the legacy of our good works and the loving relationships we leave behind. There is no question that it is important to live a productive and successful life but it is more important to teach and show by our actions those surrounding us throughout our lives the value of loving, respecting, and appreciating family and friends.

In closing, *acceptance* or compromise should be viewed as a success, *not a failure*. We must realize when we make a decision to accept change that this acceptance allows us to stop resisting the inevitable and enables us to begin the process of using logic, giving us the ability to analyze the *action/reaction* process responsible for bringing about change. In other words, rather than constantly resisting change, we can reposition ourselves to analyze why the change was necessary, how it impacts us directly, and then make the necessary adjustments to apply that change in a way that causes us the least amount of turmoil within our daily lives. By using acceptance, we can incorporate the *aura/power* method to seek harmony with an ever-changing world.

CHAPTER 15

PERSONAL CENSORSHIP

Censorship is a word used quite often in America and is said to be one of the earliest tenants during the writing of our Constitution and the founding of our country. The early framers of our Constitution understood that without free speech our society could be influenced or controlled by our government. We must remember that in early America the main source of information was the newspaper. If we review early American history, we find many stories of a conflict between the growth of government and the fight to assure the rights of a free press and free speech. American citizens today are living in a very different environment than our forefathers did. We must contend with the explosion of a technological revolution that is fueling the media, the Internet, and social networking. It is incredible that technology has given us the ability to know what happens around the world as it is happening. However, we also need to recognize that this information revolution can also be incredibly dangerous to our society if our media becomes biased or has an ideological agenda guiding its messaging. The beginnings of reporting news were built from folks choosing journalism as their career who lived by a code of ethics that assured the public true facts in their reporting of an incident or event. Journalists knew the importance of committing to honest reporting so that ordinary citizens and the nation received true unfiltered facts about any situation. Historically the press has been an integral part of helping the country solve many injustices for people who may not have had a voice without them

Throughout this book I've mentioned the importance of studying the messaging our families receive and being cautious when we see our government empowering media monopolies or groups of wealthy elites to gain control of our lives by influencing the messaging we receive. Research tells us that at onetime America had 185 independently owned media outlets (*i.e., newspaper, magazine, news stations, radio*). Internet sources now report that this number has been reduced to seven independent media sources.

I mentioned earlier that throughout America small businesses are being consumed by *corporate giants,* and the media is no exception to the rule. What's different about the consolidation of the media is that the seven remaining providers are divided according to partisan ideology, basically "sold" to us as news with a political slant. What I mean by partisan media is that the commentary they provide has been divided into purely a *left or right* ideological viewpoint. The subliminal messaging provided by cable news is done similarly to Hollywood's messaging system through their network programming. If we look closely we will see that cable news has been divided into *left or right* political commentary, basically selling messaging for the politicians they support.

This should alarm every American, but the population that has been impacted the most from this trend are the *Millennials* and the recent *immigrants* coming to America. The reason I pay particular attention to these two groups is that America's future regarding *freedom and independence* will soon be in their hands. It is critically important that they are aware of the consequences our nation faces if our media is used for nothing more than *a messaging system* promoting propaganda from a political power that is tainted or being coerced by corporate money.

Younger generations must understand that in order for America to remain free, the protection of our first amendment is critically important. The consequences of abusing the first amendment to the Constitution by the media are that we will become a people without moral clarity or a united family structure. If we allow one side of this *left or right* political viewpoint to overpower the other, we will have lost the ability to have a balanced future and outlook by means of the power of open debate.

Depending on your viewpoint regarding the discussion of censorship, we are beginning to see arguments addressing what *should or should not* be considered in this discussion. What amazes me is there is a plethora of people that use and distribute pornography with the belief it should be untouched with any form of censorship... yet many of these same people wholeheartedly support the formation of a *PC culture* responsible for silencing other citizens that might disagree with their opinion regarding America's future.

In order for us to continue the conversation regarding mental health, I would like to change the conversation to what I refer to as **"*Personal Censorship."*** Please stay with me, this is not an attempt to convert our conversation into a moral, religious or self-righteous judgment... my only concern is to bring logic to the debate in order to protect the mental health to us as a nation.

When I discuss *personal censorship,* it must be done with a logical approach. So please continue with an open mind so together we can analyze the facts using logic to learn what kinds of programs we should consider acceptable or readily available for *our children's viewing.* I believe as citizens we can avoid partisanship bickering spurred on by those who have much to lose when it pertains to the discussion of potential censorship.

Let's begin this conversation by discussing the availability of pornography on the Internet. I am not a pious person who is attempting to address the subject from a moral point of view. My approach is more from the perspective of our mental health as it pertains to relationships. Many marital relationships throughout America have become weakened because of the unreal expectations communicated by the media and the self-indulgence created by the easy access to pornography. At one time people went to an adult book store to purchase an adult magazine or video. Now this material and more is easily accessible by turning on the TV.

For some Americans the availability to pornography may prove harmless to their mental health or their relationships. For others it can completely disrupts their lives, causing a catastrophic reaction of being out of control because they can think of nothing else. These are the folks carrying the label porn addict. This addiction to pornography is no different than having an addiction to alcohol or drugs. Addictions consume your life and your mind and leave little room for a person to live normally.

This addiction stems from the personality traits we discussed earlier and our ability to control the overpowering urges they bring. Before we continue, it is important to mention to those struggling with addiction that you are not alone! Many people (some may be people close to you) struggle with some form of addiction, although some may be good at hiding it. We can empathize with you since *who the hell wouldn't suffer from an addiction* with the constant onslaught of negative messaging out there!

In order to stay on the path of mental health and avoid a debate regarding what should or *should not be protected* by the first amendment, I would like to discuss this subject in terms of what is best for the structure of our families and our country. Pornography is big business and has lots of money backing it to assure that it remains available. I might even concede that it may be better if it does stay because without it we might have an escalation of sex crimes. What I desire most is to help those suffering from addiction, to understand why it is you are suffering, and to let you know that *you are in fact being set up to fail!*

What we must decide collectively is whether we are going to continue to allow the *advertisers of evil* to continue baiting us into a life filled with guilt or one that causes us to respond without thinking to the weakened state of our most vulnerable personality traits. Or will we use what we've learned about ourselves to get in touch with *who we are* by identifying our strengths and weaknesses, helping us to combat these daily stresses within our lives. If we continue to be distracted and allow free rein to our impulses brought on by subliminal messaging, will we ever discover our *gift* that allows us to achieve our potential?

These are the questions each one of us must ask ourselves if not for us then for our children. I have used pornography as an example that affects the stability of our mental health and possibly causes disruption in a loving relationship with our partner. We are adults, and ultimately the things we do will either impact our mental stability or we must learn to somehow find peace with our actions. A child, on the other hand, deserves a chance to grow up without being impacted or tainted by seeing an abusive relationship on a computer screen. Allowing a young child to have access to pornography can create catastrophic conditions that may be irreparable as they enter adulthood.

My plea to the parents or guardians of America's children is to consider what we've discussed in the *Family Matters* chapter. We must define early on the *strengths and weaknesses* of our children, helping them to find their *gift* for the purpose of creating *balance* for the challenges they will face. Parents, not Hollywood or our government, must decide what is good for their children in order to secure a solid foundation for them, The *energy/aura* we discussed earlier and the loving exchange between two people in a relationship can only happen if our children have balanced personality traits, allowing them to be open and receptive to others.

In the past, it has been our religious institutions that have had a great deal to do with creating a moral society. Many Americans today classify themselves as either agnostic or nonreligious. Religion no longer plays as active role in our lives as it did in the past. However, it is not my intention to promote my religious beliefs here. I ask you as fellow citizens that you consider the idea of instilling *personal censorship* in your homes as one of the solutions to protecting your soul and your children's future.

There is no need for us to find agreement on religion or to debate censoring the first amendment. I hope we can find agreement together as we realize that the *advertisers of evil* are willing to sell products that negatively affect our nation's soul, and they should not be allowed to affect the personal health of the people we love. Our only way to defeat this force is to become balanced citizens in search of creating positive *energy/aura* with other fellow citizens and to let others know that they are not alone with their struggles of finding peace and a strong mental health.

I believe that *personal censorship* can be taught during the *weed pulling* process of our children's lives. Throughout this writing we've discussed maintaining our balance, and I have used addiction to pornography as an example in order to emphasize the danger that this messaging can create by stimulating our impulses and our overzealous personality traits. We are without question under attack and in order for us to get through these daily stresses we must have knowledge of what is happening and the tools needed to help us succeed in maintaining our balance.

I would like to be clear; I am in no way implying we change the first amendment. I am merely stating that if we stand without a *moral foundation or a personal censorship* without a basic understanding of the things that can promote danger for our children and our society, then we shall surely see our demise as a nation. The strength of our country has been the legitimacy of our legal system and the moral character of our citizens. In order to assure the future generations of this great nation a chance to have the American Dream, it is upon us to make sure we pull the weeds!

CHAPTER 16

TERROR

When it comes to love...I've heard people use the term *"Love is in the eye of the beholder."* This term is used when people can't explain why someone they know has chosen a person to be their soul mate. Terror, similar to *love as a strong feeling,* is also something that can be described as something *"in the eye of the beholder."*

For some of you *fear* starts the minute you step out of your home. For others the feeling of *fear* may start when you enter a busy parking lot at the grocery store and the anxiety mounts as you become frustrated looking for a parking spot. You begin to question whether you should go into the store because you fear that the anxious feeling might overwhelm you as you navigate your way through the busy isles and the overabundance of products.

There are many Americans out there struggling from what the medical establishment has termed *panic attacks*. First, I believe it important for those of you suffering from the terror of having a *panic attack* to know that you are not alone. People all over America are suffering from some form of *panic*. Some are simply better at disguising the symptoms, having developed techniques to deal with going over the edge to pure *panic*.

What the medical industry has learned about *panic attacks* is although the person experiencing the symptoms of an attack may feel as though he or she will pass out or possibly die from what seems to be a heart attack, the good news is that very few people actually die from this overwhelming sensation of panic. I mention this with utmost care because those suffering from *panic attacks* find little comfort from me saying no need to worry you will more than likely be fine!

For me the knowledge of knowing I was not a freak when dealing with a difficult problem and that many others were suffering from similar feelings gave me relief. When you are facing the terror that accompanies *panic,* hearing that other people are dealing with something similar and that none of them are dying from the process, this should at least comfort you in knowing that it is not life threatening.

I will attempt to apply logic as to why you are feeling this sense of losing control, thus causing the feeling of panic. It has everything to do with what we have discussed throughout this book. First, it begins with overstimulation of messaging, expectations of oneself, peer pressure, career pressure, political sensationalism, terrorist attacks...the list goes on and on as to what we are exposed to daily!

We discussed in an earlier chapter the question of *"who are you,"* attempting to define your *personality traits* and your *gift.* I've found through years of management that there are two additional categories I have used to define employees. To keep this simple, what I've found is there is the *"me first person"* and the *"you first person."* Both of these traits can be effective within a business but they are totally different (opposites). The *"me first person"* is less prone to suffer from emotional setbacks because their view of things is if an occurrence does not affect them, why should they bother caring? Consequently, they are able to dismiss any emotional distress because it is out of sight out of mind! It is entirely different for the *"you first person"* because this person has a much higher emotional IQ. He or she has the ability to sense everything happening within a room and is generally worried how an event that occurred might affect everyone! This person is much more prone to *panic* because they have a much wider energy field absorbing feeling, fears, and changes.

The great news is if you are a *"you first person,"* the world is a better place because of you! The bad news is that because of your tendency to be a tad hypersensitive and because of the overabundance of stimuli flooding your mind daily, you are more prone to becoming overwhelmed and having a *panic attack.* This is where we must get back to *"do you control your mind or does your mind control you,"* because if at that moment you are not in control of your mind and can see and feel the plethora of emotion of the people around you, you will probably be overwhelmed and have the potential to have a panic attack,

I will continue later on in the chapter on how to help the *"you first people"* better understand how they can defeat the onset of panic attacks, but first let's discuss why they are having panic attacks. If you have an emotional IQ and ultrasensitive receptors, all the subliminal messaging we receive and have detailed may put *"the you first people"* in a state of emotional overload.

Another important element is the threat of *terror/terrorism* happening here in the United States and around the world. What the terrorists have been able to accomplish is to put our childhood boogie man back in our closet. Unfortunately, the power of *thought* we learned as children to eliminate this fear will have no effect removing this boogie man in the adult. If we as a nation cannot agree that we must turn on the light in the closet and physically remove this boogie man, it will continue to wreak havoc on our nation's mental health.

If you recall, I started this book by discussing how many of us Americans wake up each morning and tune into their favorite choice of *local or cable* news. If we reflect back 25 years ago, it is incredible how little we knew then as a nation regarding what was happening worldwide, and we most assuredly did not know *"the news"* as it was happening!

The way I see it the power of today's technology can only go two ways. *It can either empower us to bring justice and freedom to the world or it can trap us into a cage similar to a lab rat scurrying through a maze of barriers with our direction being determined by technical scientists!* Please take a moment to consider my last statement. As we continue as a country, technology will either empower or destroy our freedoms... we must make sure that it is us as a collective unified citizenship that decides our future.

Many of you may review that last paragraph thinking I am going off the deep end with my comments of destruction, but please hear me out because I am going to take you through a journey of our action/reaction process explaining my concerns. In order to understand the danger of the boogie man in our closet, we must review how our nation is functioning as a whole, using technology to help elevate the progress of a changing ideology within our nation. I promise this is not going to go into politics, but it will walk around the surface of how the political machine has used technology to advance its cause.

I referred earlier to the creation of walls brought about by the *technical scientists*, making it sound as though this is a story out of science fiction. I assure you if we as a nation do not pay attention to the details, this *science fiction* will become our reality. I am going to dissect this into four groups: government, media, terror, and last but and not least the mental health and freedom of you the citizen. If we start with a review of our government and its functions, we realize it is a representative government elected by the citizens. Its main responsibilities are to protect our citizens from eminent danger from foreign lands and to create laws to help govern a civil society. What many Americans do not realize is that most of our government is composed of lawyers who have spent their entire careers twisting and reshaping the law to achieve outcomes that are favorable to their clients or perhaps their business.

If we think of this in numbers, on average Congress writes approximately 7000 new bills each year, passing on average around 700 bills. If these bills are enacted into law, this translates into 700 additional changes or potential restrictions to you as a citizen.

If we travel into science fiction, creating a narrative from the *Twilight Zone,* we would see giant figures of the *people in Congress and other areas of government* standing over our cage displaying us as tiny insignificant people like the rats in their cages under the observation of the government scientist! If we then visualize the 700 new bills becoming law each year and then envision them placing each new law within the rat's cage as additions to the walls already guiding them within the maze, we can clearly see how each rat would be confused by a pathway to their life now being obstructed by each new wall (or law).

As we have seen in science the rats will eventually adjust to the additional walls, finding passage to the other side and ultimately locating their water and food for survival. I understand that the visual I've used to represent our elected government is somewhat harsh, but the consequences of their continuous need to create new and different laws for you and me are very real and have similar results to my description of the rats in the cage. Remember my goal is always to help you understand that your problems are mostly created for you through the ongoing effect of change!

Now it is time to discuss our media and how they have impacted our lives. These are the folks displaying and sensationalizing the things we view and are also the main contributors to putting the boogie man back in our closet! We've discussed the impact of advertising and the change within our network programing and its impact upon our family's mental health. We must now turn our discussion to the media's use of power to spread a divided ideology to citizens along with heightening the narrative of terror. Please do not misconstrue my message. I do not believe the media is actively attempting to hurt us or that they are conspiring with government to bring down our nation. However, I do believe that because their business profits are based on ratings, creating sensationalism for the viewing audience has become the predominant way that they attract viewers and expand their profits.

If we look back at the creation of new laws brought to us by government and combine this with sensationalized messages from our media displayed daily on television or whatever source you use to obtain your news, we can deduce that what has happened to the average family from this combined attack is its action/reaction effect, causing many families to take refuge within the four walls of their homes.

In other words, because we are living in a *state of fear,* our government reacts to this by creating more do's and don'ts (laws) for you. Also, because our media constantly displays for us the sensationalism of horrifying news and terrorism from around the globe, the action/reaction to this fills people with anxiety and fear. And secondary reaction to this is that we hold our children close to us fearful of what may happen to them when they leave the safety of their homes.

My purpose for bringing this up is not to cause more fear or to depict the news we receive as garbage but to continue the narrative... *who would not have anxiety* with what we face as citizens on a daily basis. Again, my concern is you and your mental health and the impact this is having on us as a collective nation. It is critical we get the truth out to our citizens... it is not the American people who brought this fear and damage to our nation but the *savage work of those corrupting our country for the purpose of power and financial rewards!*

If we reflect back to our childhood we can remember how we got past the fear of the boogie man in our closet. The first thing my parents did was to shine a light in the closet in order to show me what I thought I saw was merely an illusion. Then they focused on positive things, telling me I had nothing to worry about, it was safe. They took the time to remind me of the good things that happened that day, attempting to distract my thoughts from the worry or fear of that damn boogie man!

If we review the work of our network news media and compare how they report terror, we see that their actions are in direct contrast to how our parents handled the terror in our childhood lives. In addition, if we look beyond reports of terrorism and examine the other news they bring to us, the results are just as frightening.

My point is not to compare today's news media to our parents but to point out the solution our parents used to rid us of our crisis. There is no question that America and the rest of the world have a *real boogie man,* seeking the destruction of our freedom. Collectively as citizens we need to find agreement on how we can best slay this dragon. However, we should first also ask the question of whether there is anything positive that the *news media* can find to report on regarding what's happening within America throughout the day?

I believe that the latest census established that there are approximately 320million Americans. The tragic news stories we receive daily represent the smallest part of what happens within our country each day. For instance, *Fox News* has decided to use the devastating murder rate of Chicago's African American community to paint a picture of Chicago as a disaster zone. The truth is there is a small section within Chicago proper that has a high crime rate for the people living in in that area, but it is a small reflection of a large city that has good things happening every day.

There may be some of you who disagree asking how will we ever change what is happening in these communities if we do not draw attention to these atrocities. I agree and believe we should report the atrocities in high crime communities along with reporting terrorist attacks when they happen, but we must also hear the *good news* happening each day! If we use the census to break down daily tragedies and compare them to the number of good things happening in America every day, we would find that 95% of the things that could be reported within our nation would be positive and 5% would represent the negative.

My major point is that our media has chosen to use the 5% of tragic news to represent 100% of the news they report. There may be a few local media outlets in small towns that still report on the brave fireman rescuing a cat from a tree, but it comes across loud and clear that cable news has collectively decided to keep America in a state of fear and despair and decided to keep the boogie man alive and well in our closet.

Unfortunately, this boogie man we speak of is now being harvested from within our society. We must now also look at unfortunate conditions developing within our families as a result of malignant advertising, in particular the selling of their products at the expense of our children's innocent but impressionable minds. We have already discussed the importance of *personal censorship,* using pornography and its bad influences as an example. . We will now examine the video game industry and its effect of desensitizing our children's minds to the blood and guts of killing.

If we go back to our earlier discussion regarding the value of the food we eat and its effects on both our physical and mental health and we continue the conversation as it pertains to the educational information we digest, I believe we will come to the same conclusion that they both matter! The latest in food innovation has brought us the ability to take fruits and vegetables and grind them into a liquid and then pour them into a glass, giving us a powerful smoothie filled with nutrition! There is no question that those choosing to live a lifestyle of healthy eating and regular exercise are receiving greater health benefits that contribute to a longer lasting and healthier life compared to those who do not.

It is time to for us to create another visual by making a smoothie out of the products and information we have been forced to digest. Let's open up the blender and put in the sensationalized propaganda of *identity politics* we receive from our politicians. Then we must turn to Hollywood and our television network programming in order to stir in the action-packed movies with the plots of mass killings or the amazing graphics of zombies showing beheadings or devouring another human being. Last, we cannot complete this information smoothie without including our home video games that teach our children how to emulate those or admire those who use their imagination, skills, and weapons to kill people on their TV screens in their homes.

Once we blend this barrage of daily exposure to information products, we should add spice order to make sure the taste is not too bitter. In order to spruce up the visual our families digest, let's toss in the use of marijuana and other street drugs. Just in case a few kids get overstimulated, the pharmaceutical industry can create more drugs that can help dull the senses to the dramatic impact of overstimulation.

I ask every reader to carefully consider what has been put into our families' blender and once we've digested the impact, we should then turn the conversation to America's second amendment. How and why has the conversation regarding the second amendment become the only part of the discussion to solving this dilemma of terror happening within America society?

How many of our children are sitting at home in front to their television sets or other devices having access to or playing these video games of death and destruction while their parents work? And how many parents believe the television is a great way to keep their children busy and safe from the exposure to the dangers outside their door we see broadcasted on network news?

Have we allowed a toxic cocktail to be brewed in our homes? Is the solution to merely take guns out of the hands of our citizens but allow these *advertisers of evil* to continue with these dangerous and destructive games and programs? We all know the answer to these questions and yet we've continued to allow both our media and our politicians to divide and distract us by feeding the 5% bad news and keeping us from the 95% good news!

We must ask ourselves what is their end game? Is it to keep growing the size of security provided to us from a federal government and taking it away from our citizens? Does this end game include removing all weapons for self-protection from society and asking us to rely on their government for total security? Will we through our fear accept the walls of security from our government and be content to let them restrict our freedoms? Will we live under an imposed curfew becoming controlled by the restrictions of a multitude of laws put in place to protect us from ourselves?

It is time we must put a stop to this control and t realize that *you and your children are being set up to fail,* The only chance we have of removing this boogie man from our closet is to stop the *advertisers of evil* and the *merchandisers of madness* from having unsupervised access into our homes with their products of destruction. Remember our earlier discussion about the importance of parents' pulling the weeds from our children's gardens so that we can protect their mental health and provide them with a foundation that will help carry them through life's trials and tribulations. In order for us to have children who's mental health is built from strength, we must participate throughout their lives paying attention to what our societal leaders deem acceptable for the public in order to ensure our kids *are not being set up to fail*

CHAPTER 17

WEATHERING THE STORM

Throughout life all of us will experience ups and downs. Some of us will suffer trials and tribulations far worse than others, but regardless of our stress we must always recognize that each of us is built with an inner strength to **Weather the Storm.** We hear these phrases passed down from courageous people who have lived to tell the story of their *fight for survival,* and many of those stories became a guiding light for future generations.

In order to create another visual let's consider our elected government as Captains at the helm steering a great ship (naming this ship) *"America"* and to complete this visualization let's imagine the Captains of "America" navigating us directly into an iceberg, similar to the fate of the *Titanic!* The term "weathering the storm" came from traveling the sea and was on every Captain's mind each time they took their courageous journey across vast oceans in ships many of us today might not call seaworthy. They knew the risk as they entered the open waters, knowing they would need to see the preemptive signs delivered by *Mother Nature* in order to help them decide what the turbulence of each journey might be. The skilled Captain's developed strategies to position their ships when the *high winds and waves began,* giving orders to the shipmates to batten down the hatches in order to *weather the storm!*

What the phrase meant at that time was that the only thing going through the Captain's mind was to properly position his ship into the wind and waves, giving him the best chance to prevent capsizing his ship. Regardless of your age, most of us know the popular song done by Reo Speed Wagon's *"Ridin the Storm Out"* The musician's lyrics help us to better understand what the captain and crew were doing while they waited for the storm to pass. If we compare the sea captains journey to the life of a coal miner who survived a collapsed tunnel, we realize at the peak of the coal miner's fight for life within the dark collapsed tunnel, the only hope was to keep digging and to hold on long enough, hoping he might **see light at the end of the tunnel!**

My goal throughout this book has been to deliver the good news that you are not alone. Whether you suffer from anxiety, panic attacks, depression, financial struggles, heartbreak, or loss of a parent or a child, we must always enter each battle of adversity with the knowledge that *"this too shall pass."* These valuable phrases are timeless words of wisdom passed on to us as *gifts* from those who have endured. What should be learned from their meaning is that these powerful words of wisdom came from conditions of *survival and not death.* In other words, they were meant to build strength in others, inspiring us with the hope and fortitude we need to survive our trials and tribulations; also helping us to understand that we are not alone and our problems won't last forever.

Because I fall into the *"you first person"* category, I generally do not like to talk about myself in a boastful way. If I do, it is always for the purpose of giving others strength. I will share enough about my life to let you know that although I am successful, it has not been an easy path to accomplishment. As I mentioned earlier, one of my *gifts* has been the ability to battle my way through whatever life delivers, understanding that times of turbulence will come but if I hang in there and maintain my balance I should be able to *weather the storm and ride it out.*

In my first book "United We Stand...Don't Tread on USA," in the Prologue I shared information about the author with the reader. My education came from *"the street of hard knocks"* and *"I have a master's degree in what is referred to as life."* This no doubt is a play on words, but it is also the truth! There are many people diligently going to school educating themselves in their chosen profession and believing that once their education is complete, their path to success is all but assured. However, once they leave school and enter into the competition of finding a job, they began to realize that the work they put in at school had the sole purpose of providing them with a foundation and that they had to continue learning the things school could not teach until they were participating in the real world!

I will spare you most of the details of my life, but I thought it important to share part of my journey through *what is now referred to as the "Great Recession."* Prior to the recession my brother and I had spent 20 years building a successful business. We both began our careers working in different but similar businesses in the construction industry. Each of us started in the trenches, fighting our way to become of greater value to our employers. My brother was more gregarious by nature and more of a natural salesman, and as I mentioned earlier...I had discovered that my *gift* was the love of building and managing people.

Both my brother and I were extremely independent by nature and wanted more from life than working for someone else, so over time we came together as partners and built a successful business in the Chicago area. As with any business it started small, and since we remained committed to our customers' satisfaction, word of mouth spread that we were an excellent company and our business grew by leaps and bounds each year.

During the company's successful growth period we worked hard at building a team by empowering our employees, similar to the strategy I used on the kids' baseball team. The key to our success was that we encouraged our employees to reach for the stars...letting them know that as long as they gave us their best effort regardless of mistakes, we would reward them and fix our problems as a team. We taught our employees the importance of collectively *"competing against the competition"* and not against each other. This led to success and growth and offered opportunities to advance within the company.

The partnership has worked between my brother and me because we've worked diligently at allowing each other the space needed to be successful with our independent *gifts*. We have been extremely careful to assure that our *energy/aura* was shared in order to create a positive influence on those around us. The result of this was that we were able to empower our employees by letting them know they had much to do with the company's success.

When people in the construction industry become successful, many owners tend to invest in real estate because it fits well with what they know. It may be buying an old building and fixing it up or buying a piece of land and constructing something new. In our case we began the process of building a real estate portfolio at the beginning of the year in 2006. We started our real estate venture with a little bit of both types, meaning we bought some old *fixer uppers* and a piece of land to build something new. At the time banks were literally handing out money for these types of ventures, and we were viewed as a highly successful business. Therefore starting our real estate company was much easier than our years of building a construction business.

Depending on the business you were in, the impact of "*The Great Recession*" struck businesses in America at different times. In other words, if you were in a financial business the impact was immediate. The negative impact for our business did not start until year end 2008 owing to having a full year's worth of backlog remaining from 2007 sales. When the recession began we actually felt good at the time, thinking we were positioned well enough to *weather the storm* if the recession was similar to others in the past. What followed after the financial collapse of December 2007 was a chain of events that put businesses and families all over America through seven years of pure hell!

I will try just to share enough to give you the impact of the recession on us personally. Due to the financial collapse, the new building we had constructed costing us several million dollars remained empty for three long years, causing a depletion of cash within our businesses. What infuriated me the most was that the banks responsible for the crash because they had carelessly handed out money to anyone with a heartbeat were now responsible for shutting down the loaning process to everyone with the exception of the very wealthy who didn't need to borrow! Our new building remained empty because there were no businesses remaining in need of or that could afford to rent space. Additionally, because we owned and operated a construction business, we were severely affected because the banks had completely shut down lending money to main street, thereby completely stopping any possibility of construction. The end result for us was a near collapse of our construction business.

In order to explain the extent of their recklessness and its impact on our business, in the year 2007 our company billed 37 million dollars in completed work; after the devastation imposed on America from the banking industry our business billed a whopping total of 11 million dollars in 2010! Those of you not familiar with business are probably thinking *"you still billed 11 million,"* what are you complaining about? However, the cost to keep our business open using minimal employees along with no salary for my brother or myself in the year 2010 was 12.5 million dollars. It does not take a mathematician to calculate that in the year 2010 not only did we have to layoff valuable employees but we lost 1.5 million dollars attempting to stay in business! We also depleted all but a few dollars remaining within our business as a result of paying bank notes on properties that had been devalued to less than 60% of what it cost us to construct. In other words, the building we paid 4.5 million dollars to construct was now being valued by the banks responsible for destroying our country at a mere 1.8 million.

Looking back upon this time in my life and attempting to understand the value of the life lessons learned, I realized it was the little battles I fought throughout my business career, always finding a way to *weather each individual storm* that gave me the strength to survive. It is important to understand that the small battles of success and failure each of us face throughout our lives should not be viewed as wasted time but as the building blocks to a foundation of strength and character, ultimately helping us to face what may be life's biggest challenge.

When I share my experience of this terrible eight-year period of time I usually start with, **"I hope like hell I never have to go through this again."** Yet I am thankful for what it taught me about myself. What I learned through my *trials and tribulations* was that each of us carries an inner strength that will help us to endure whatever challenges life brings our way. Additionally, I learned what it meant to *"weather the storm"* and why we *"save for a rainy day,"* I survived and learned the value of these phrases firsthand. It also helped me to gain perspective that the smaller things I might once have thought to be a big deal no longer seemed quite so big.

There may be some of you who may have lived through far worse conditions than my experience. In my case it was merely a condition of economics but none the less it was a tragic period of time for me and many others throughout America. I've shared this portion of my life not for the purpose of discussing who among us may have had a worse hardship but to give us a basis to work from when it comes to understanding the inner strength each of us possesses to handle difficult times when they come upon us.

Finally, what I left out of the story was while we were dealing with our economic struggle, my mother's health was reaching the end of her long struggle. Depending on your belief system, the passing of someone you love can either be filled with sadness or celebration. The passing of my mother was another sign to me that while all of us are blessed having our chance to exist on earth, we should do all we can to face life's challenges with concern but also with a smile.

For those of you facing a hardship within your life, take a moment to consider the many things we've discussed. We should never forget that the feelings we have are merely *thoughts* and that it is just as easy to think about something in a positive, productive way as it is to think about the same thing negatively. We all have the ability to control our brain and not allow our brain to control us. It requires discipline, but when we know an impulse is merely a spontaneous thought and understanding this as quickly as a thought comes, you can have another thought to control the impulse. We are not destined to follow a mind of spontaneous impulses but designed to use our minds to control *action/reaction* outcomes.

Whatever challenges you face…you must believe in your mind and your heart, *"this too shall pass."* If you are suffering from panic attacks, depression, or any other mental health ailment… something that should bring you comfort is knowing you are not alone. If something feels as though it is too big for you to handle, trust in the wisdom of those who have suffered before us letting us know that we must *weather the storm,* helping us find that *glimmer of light at the end of the tunnel!* Always remember what may seem insurmountable today will be a memory of accomplishment tomorrow!

CHAPTER 18

RELIGION

You may find it odd to see a chapter titled "Religion" within a self-help book, but I thought it is important to include religion within this discussion because as we touched on earlier, the subliminal *messaging/advertisers* needed America to be a less rigid nation if they were going to have success selling products, and religion was a major obstacle to the success of their plan. Because of the barrage of negative messaging many religious people have become weakened as they become victims of this bait, causing them to be riddled with guilt and to live a life of unhappiness or failure.

Additionally, we receive messages from a growing government as they undermine our history of America as a predominantly Judeo/Christian nation. Their pursuit of reducing the independence of America's citizens and their attempts to create citizens who are more dependent upon government entitlements sends a message to pray for perseverance in order to make it through difficult times. If we analyze the breakdown of religion reflecting back to the jobs chapter along with the chapter on anxiety, we start to realize that another benefit of destroying religion is the creation of jobs at the expense of a moral society. If people are not bound to moral character by something, they can more easily be enticed into the world of sinful things. Additionally, those people trying to be faithful to their religious doctrine and attempting to live a life free of sin are left with guilt when they fail. The result of guilt is another win for job creators and product sellers because guilt causes masses of people to seek medical/psychiatric help and their therapy and counseling generally end with a prescription for a life-numbing drug.

I will confess that I am Christian and would be remiss if I did not disclose that writing this book along with others I've written has been put in my heart by God. As I explained earlier, the success I've had during my career as a business owner has been driven by the *gift* I've received from God, which is the ability to see other people's *gifts*. Each time I write, I ponder the question of why I am writing another book, and every time I ask myself this question, I am always careful to make sure the answer is for the right reasons. The first reason is due to my respect for God, answering his call for me to write, and the second reason is driven by my care and compassion for my family and fellow citizens.

There have been many times throughout America's history that God has been involved in assuring that this nation of refuge is kept safe for the salvation of the downtrodden. We as the caretakers of this nation should take caution when the leaders we elect devote themselves to weakening the structure of a moral society. The difference between an ever-changing rule or law made by man is it is purely created on the surface and not from the heart. God's law is burned into your conscience and soul; it is not something a rich man or lawyer can debate regarding the terms of its punishment.

I understand religion is not for everyone; there are many who believe that religion is merely a philosophy designed to help keep the uneducated to remain law-abiding citizens. Stephen Hawking, the originator of the big bang theory, recently relented from his theory of believing a perfect set of circumstances happened in order to create what we know as earth. He now believes nothing is perfect, and that the creation of earth was done from imperfection. I can't help but rub it in a little to the *big bang believers*, but God who gave us his only begotten son to save us from the imperfections of mankind tells us he already knew the hypothesis of Mr. Hawking's conclusion.

Since we know there are folks like Mr. Hawking out there who do not believe in the concept of a God as having created earth and man. We also know there is a rise in the belief that religion is merely a philosophy created to control the uneducated. I am not qualified or interested in attempting to change anyone's view regarding their beliefs in creation. To pursue the answer of what happened by tracing what is written or what is said would be an undertaking leading to nothing but frustration. At the end of the day religion boils down to one thing, which is faith. Many people misconstrue the meaning of the word faith and spend countless hours studying the creation of religion in order to better secure their faith. We all must find our own way within the life we are given, and in order to secure my faith I decided to believe in Christ not based on evidence but by the main premise of the word faith. Faith is defined as believing in something even though you have no concrete proof to support its cause. It is blind and it is trust and regardless of the arguments for or against it is a decision you make because you know in your heart it is right for you.

Whether you believe in Christ or not…if you know enough about his ministry and know it was based on love, compassion, and living a moral life, it is difficult to find holes in the value of what he preached. If we were to use the written word and its subliminal message as it was meant to be received (love without prejudice) the world would be a far better place.

As I mentioned earlier, it is not my purpose to convince anyone on their religious beliefs, but I would like to continue on my concern for our mental stability as a nation through the barrage of subliminal messaging. If we make a comparison of our nation in the present era to the time of Christ, I believe it's fair to conclude that if Jesus were here today, his view of America would be similar to his actions at the Temple Mount when he decided to overturn the tables of the *money exchangers* who were selling sacrificial lambs in order to properly celebrate Passover. When Jesus tipped over the tables filled with shekels he stated, "not in my Father's house." He was aware that the celebration of Passover had been corrupted by wealthy religious leaders using a system of money on sacred ground to manipulate and profit from God's people.

America has become a melting pot of different cultures and religions. Even though it was formed by predominantly white European settlers coming from nations of Christian origin, these early settlers were not free from religious differences because of the multitude of different Christian denominations. So from the beginning whether they were Catholic, Lutheran, Methodist, Baptist, or Seventh Day Adventist, the early settlers had to submit to a common agreement in order to unify and respect their *"different yet same"* beliefs that Jesus was the son of God who died for the sins of mankind. They elected to find agreement and tolerance using Christ as the unifying factor of peace.

Please do not misconstrue my message. It is not my intent to convince anyone to become Christian; my hope is regardless of your choice of religion, you will find within it what I've found in mine: peace, love of family, faith to believe in something without proof, and to seek harmony with all people. When we see priests, pastors, and evangelicals arguing their position and representing their denomination as the only path to Christ, I find it hard to believe that Jesus would agree with the prejudice and judgment coming from many of our religious institutions. If we compare how Christ lived his time on earth dedicating his life to kindness, love, and making the world a better place by being an example, we see that many religious institutions no longer follow Christ's work.

I close my thoughts regarding religion by once more reminding you that we are faced with the daily onslaught of subliminal messaging delivered to us through the *mass media* and a *divisive government*. The attempt by these messengers is to weaken the power of our religious convictions in order to encourage the masses to follow their impulses and to buy their products. Additionally, we have an ideology within government that is aimed at lessening our independence and removing the internal strength we gain from our religion, thus creating a citizen reliant upon government for its provisions. America is defined throughout the world as a nation of free people having the right to choose a religion of choice and to speak freely with an open mind. We must continue to be an example to the world, proving it is possible for a citizenship to collectively live together as one nation.

CHAPTER 19

THE FUTURE FOR
WE THE PEOPLE

The success of our nation does not depend on government, technology, ideology, mass media, or any of these powerful forces or messaging systems infiltrated into our daily existence. The success of America will be decided by the mental strength and stability of our citizens and our families. As a nation we must come together and realize the importance of the *energy/aura* we give and receive, strengthen our relationships with others, communicate effectively with our children, and help others lost in the abyss from the dangers of subliminal messaging.

It is critically important now more than ever that we stop the divisive politics and come together as Americans in order to preserve the freedoms we hold as a nation. We should discuss the problems of America's future without the radical rhetoric and bipartisan politics. We must understand and respect that America has been created by a people always finding a way to come together, even when they had different opinions on how to chart our nation's future.

If we study America's past, we realize that one of the things that brought us together as a successful nation was the need to build an infrastructure and security, thus providing a sense of wellbeing to our country. Because America was built from nothing other than a common cause of a collective people seeking freedom, the thought of *being free* caused citizens from many different cultures to find *cohesion rather than division*; they realized that their collective freedom was the only chance for all to prosper independently.

Let's consider the concept that *collective freedom for all...is the only chance for citizens to prosper individually.* I believe the concept of freedom for all yet having individual success has become the stumbling block of our nation's future. As a citizenship we are receiving subliminal messaging from our government along with much of the media that tells us that a central governmental power dictating the terms of our freedom and progress is the future of America. Yet we see they are seeking to destroy our freedom in order to enhance their power.

If we use the same visualization we did earlier regarding the *energy/aura* exchange with our friends, families, and business associates and understanding the theory, we can perceive that there are people who seek to deplete your *energy/aura* in order to strengthen theirs. They use many tactics to accomplish the theft of your energy/aura: some use brute force, others seek to find your weaknesses in order to use them against you and destroy your confidence. If we're able to identify and understand how these various methods are used, it's then not difficult to visualize the tactics our government and media have used to gain power and dominance. We receive messaging from the government that they will help us with our every need, giving us the sense that self-reliance is no longer a necessity. It is important to understand that your independent spirit is your soul...it is *who you are* and surrendering your independence to anyone let alone our government is unacceptable!

In order to provide another visual, let's apply the *energy/aura* concept to our *government and media,* comparing what they are doing to us and comparing the government's tactics to what we've seen used by ordinary people attempting to consume your *energy* in order to empower theirs. If we focus on the subliminal messaging of political correctness being implemented by our government, the media, and through our educational system, we begin to realize that it is nothing more than a tool used to silence the voices of those who disagree with their ideological agenda.

The result the politicians gain from the use of political correctness is a division of our citizens done through the use of identity politics. The object of identity politics is to divide our citizenship into separate collective groups. Rather than bringing us together as one nation under the concept of freedom, their goal is to divide us into groups for the purpose of decreasing our strength of oneness or common cause. If we can visualize our *energy/aura* that surrounds us and use the same visualization of an *energy/aura* surrounding our *government/media,* we would see the efforts to deplete our *energy* and to create an all-powerful government.

Much of our youth has been conditioned to accept government as the solution to our freedom. However, the premise of America set by our founders was that was in order to remain a free independent people it must be understood and agreed upon that a growing centralized government was a danger to the concept of a *free* independent people. Regardless of our political affiliations we must consider the thought that no matter how much we may disagree with another person's opinion, do any of us honestly believe that seeking none of their input can have value in obtaining an outcome that will satisfy all? I believe this question has become the number one issue for our nation.

I bring this question to us as citizens not for the purpose of more divisive language but to remind us that America came into existence because of the will of its citizens seeking to be free from an oppressive King. As we continue asking ourselves the question *"what is the future for we the people?,"* I ask you to step away from the daily subliminal messaging delivered to us from our *government/media* and take a moment to analyze with logic the *action/reaction* to better understand the results of their deeds. America's future and freedom depend on a mentally fit citizenship finding agreement on how to we solve the debt and division brought to us from the leaders of our country.

The title of this book implies a question, "Are you being set up to fail?" I believe that most of you have come to the conclusion that *yes, we are in fact being set up to fail* in every conceivable way! Each day we go on as a people listening to messaging filled with terror, doubt, indecision, and divisiveness. Our media reports crisis after crisis, doing all they can to sensationalize every event or story. Our politicians work at dividing us as a people pointing out our differences rather than discussing what we have in common. The mental health of our nation is suffering, and it is for good reason. It is time for America's citizens to come together as a unified people in order to halt the messages of division and destruction perpetrated upon us by politicians. We must come together as sensible people realizing that these onslaughts have been an attack on our normalcy, and it is up to us to stop them in order to secure a future based on freedom and independence for our children.

It may be unrealistic for me to hope that everyone who has read the theory of sharing *energy/aura* will understand the importance of how this sharing with others on equal terms could clearly benefit us significantly as a whole. The world will always have *energy givers and energy stealers* but if each of us can convince even a small percentage of our family and friends of our mission through our own subliminal messaging, we can help build and transfer the flow of our positive *energy/aura,* thus improving the mental health of the people we know and love.

In closing, I ask that you please not misconstrue my message as an attempt to create a utopian society. The concept of *energy/aura* is to help you visualize and understand the motivation behind *personality/characteristic* traits and the impact they can have on our mental state of mind. We can make a difference in the lives of the people we love and those we come in contact with daily. My hope is as more people become aware of *who they are* by learning what their *gift from God is,* they can find peace within their comfort zone, ultimately reducing their anxiety.

My hope is that I have enlightened you on the idea that effective parenting comes from being involved in your child's life, helping them to identify and understand their personality traits and to find balance in their lives. We must also remember that all humanity has problems and that we are not alone in our struggles. We've learned how to identify when others seek to weaken us through the theft of our *energy/aura,* giving us the tools to cope with the discovery of *"who you are"* and to strengthen our *"gift."* In this way we can assure you the ability to remain within a balanced state of mental health.

I hope you've learned that we are *"being set up to fail"* by a system that places more importance on the sale of goods and services than the mental health of its citizens. We are not crazy... we are in fact being overloaded with subliminal messaging all for the sake of selling products. We are being attacked by a messaging system delivered through government, Hollywood, and the media that the idea of being a free independent people is an ideology of the past; for those who disagree, they will use their power to try silence you by the use of political correctness!

We must decide as a collective citizenship if we will cave into the *advertisers of evil* allowing them to weaken our resolve as a free people and surrender our power of independence or shall we remain the strength of America by sending them a message stating *the independent spirit of the American people is not for sale!*